Generative AI for Full-Stack Development

AI Empowered Accelerated Coding

Shantanu Baruah
Nitara Baruah

Apress®

Generative AI for Full-Stack Development: AI Empowered Accelerated Coding

Shantanu Baruah
Somerset, NJ, USA

ISBN-13 (pbk): 979-8-8688-2073-1 ISBN-13 (electronic): 979-8-8688-2074-8
https://doi.org/10.1007/979-8-8688-2074-8

Copyright © 2025 by Shantanu Baruah

This work is subject to copyright. All rights are reserved by the Publisher, whether the whole or part of the material is concerned, specifically the rights of translation, reprinting, reuse of illustrations, recitation, broadcasting, reproduction on microfilms or in any other physical way, and transmission or information storage and retrieval, electronic adaptation, computer software, or by similar or dissimilar methodology now known or hereafter developed.

Trademarked names, logos, and images may appear in this book. Rather than use a trademark symbol with every occurrence of a trademarked name, logo, or image we use the names, logos, and images only in an editorial fashion and to the benefit of the trademark owner, with no intention of infringement of the trademark.

The use in this publication of trade names, trademarks, service marks, and similar terms, even if they are not identified as such, is not to be taken as an expression of opinion as to whether or not they are subject to proprietary rights.

While the advice and information in this book are believed to be true and accurate at the date of publication, neither the authors nor the editors nor the publisher can accept any legal responsibility for any errors or omissions that may be made. The publisher makes no warranty, express or implied, with respect to the material contained herein.

Managing Director, Apress Media LLC: Welmoed Spahr
Acquisitions Editor: Anandadeep Roy
Editorial Project Manager: Jessica Vakili

Distributed to the book trade worldwide by Springer Science+Business Media New York, 1 New York Plaza, New York, NY 10004. Phone 1-800-SPRINGER, fax (201) 348-4505, e-mail orders-ny@springer-sbm.com, or visit www.springeronline.com. Apress Media, LLC is a Delaware LLC and the sole member (owner) is Springer Science + Business Media Finance Inc (SSBM Finance Inc). SSBM Finance Inc is a **Delaware** corporation.

For information on translations, please e-mail booktranslations@springernature.com; for reprint, paperback, or audio rights, please e-mail bookpermissions@springernature.com.

Apress titles may be purchased in bulk for academic, corporate, or promotional use. eBook versions and licenses are also available for most titles. For more information, reference our Print and eBook Bulk Sales web page at http://www.apress.com/bulk-sales.

Any source code or other supplementary material referenced by the author in this book is available to readers on GitHub. For more detailed information, please visit https://www.apress.com/gp/services/source-code.

If disposing of this product, please recycle the paper

Table of Contents

About the Authors xi

About the Technical Reviewer xiii

Acknowledgments xv

Introduction xvii

Chapter 1: Introduction to Modern Web Development 1

    The Web Development Landscape 1

    Who Is This Book For? 4

    How the Book Is Structured 5

        Getting Started 5

        Web Development Foundations 5

        AI and Prompt Engineering in Practice 6

        Building the Full-Stack Application 6

        Deployment and Optimization 7

        The Future of Web Development 7

    Introducing Half Time Whistle 8

    Why Learn with Prompt Engineering? 8

    What's Next? 9

    Summary 9

Chapter 2: Environment Setup 11

    Introduction 11

    Prerequisite 11

    Install Xcode CLT 11

    Install Git 12

    Install VS Code 13

TABLE OF CONTENTS

 Setting Up GitHub 15
  Creation of GitHub Repository 15
  Create a Project Directory 16
  Setting Up VS Code to Store Source Code in GitHub 16
 MongoDB Setup 18
  Setting Up MongoDB Using the MongoDB Web Interface 19
  Creating MongoDB Using Terminal and Homebrew 22
 Summary 23

Chapter 3: Foundations of Modern Web Development 25
 Introduction 25
 The Vision Behind the Half Time Whistle 25
 Web Development Fundamentals 27
  Web Basics and Core Technologies 27
  Understanding HTML, CSS, and JavaScript 28
  Web Protocols and Architectures 29
  Introduction to Front-End and Back-End Concepts 29
  Why Full-Stack Development over WordPress or Wix? 30
 Summary 31

Chapter 4: Front-End Development 33
 Introduction 33
 HTML5 Advanced Techniques 33
 CSS Frameworks and Responsive Design 35
 JavaScript Fundamentals 37
 React.js Framework 38
 State Management with Redux 40
 Single-Page Application (SPA) Design 41
 Summary 42

Chapter 5: Database Management 43
 Introduction 43
 MongoDB Fundamentals 44

Data Modeling	46
Query Optimization	48
Database Security	50
Data Persistence Strategies	52
Summary	53

Chapter 6: Gen AI in Web Development 55

Introduction	55
Prompt Engineering Techniques	56
Zero-Shot Prompting	57
Few-Shot Prompting	57
Chain-of-Thought Prompting	60
Role-Play/Persona Prompting	62
Instruction-Based Prompting	65
Output Formatting/Constraint Prompting	68
Generated Knowledge Prompting	69
Self-Consistency Prompting	71
Tree-of-Thought Prompting	76
Comparing All Prompts	83
AI-Assisted Coding	84
Summary	85

Chapter 7: Designing a Travel Experience Website 87

Introduction	87
Home Page: An Outlet to Unlimited Adventures	87
Layered Navigation: From Continents to Regions	88
Destinations: Showcasing Individual Journeys	89
Schema Model	90
Experience Pages: Deep Dives into Each Adventure	92
Summary Experience Page	92
Detail Experience Page	94
Schema Model	95

TABLE OF CONTENTS

Design Philosophy and User Experience 99

Summary 100

Chapter 8: Application Configuration 101

Environment Default System Files 101

package.json Configuration File 102

    About the Project 102

    React Scripts 103

    ESLint Scripts 104

    Browser List 104

    Node.js Version Details 105

    Complete Code 105

package-lock.json 107

server.js 108

    Environment, Imports, and App Setup 108

    Middleware Setup 109

    Static File Serving 110

    MongoDB Connection 110

    MongoDB Schemas and Models 110

    API Route Handlers 112

    Operational and Error Handling Features 114

    Complete Code 115

    Examples of AI Prompting 119

vercel.json 123

App.js 124

    Imports 124

    The App Component and Routing Breakdown 125

    Complete Code 126

    Example of AI Prompting 128

Summary 128

TABLE OF CONTENTS

Chapter 9: The Landing Page: HomePage.js 129

Import Statements 130

Page Navigation 132

Managing Meta Data and SEO 133

Main Page Layout 134

Complete Code 138

AI Prompting 143

    Prompt 143

    Why Does This Prompt Work? 145

Home Page Stylesheet 145

Overarching Layout 146

Header and Banner Layout 146

Banner Image and Text 146

Navigation Bar 147

Main Content Area 148

Content Block Design 148

Featured Block Style 150

Footer Design 151

Media Queries: Responsive Design 151

Complete Code 152

AI Prompting 156

    Prompt for Generating This CSS 156

Summary 159

Chapter 10: Continent Page: North America 161

Imports 162

Navigation Component 164

Metadata Management 165

Header Section 166

Main Content 167

Footer Section 168

TABLE OF CONTENTS

Complete Code 168
AI Prompt 173
Summary 176

Chapter 11: Region Page 177

Key Implementation Concepts 178
Example User Flow 178
Imports 179
Component Definition: Region 179
Fetching Data with useEffect 181
fetchPlaces Function 181
PlaceComponent 183
Rendering Content 184
Content Render Structure 186
Complete Code 188
AI Prompt 194
Stylesheet for Region Component 195
The Container 196
.item 197
.item:hover 197
.item h2 198
.item-content 198
.item img 198
.item p 199
Responsive Design (Media Query for ≤768px) 199
body Style 200
Complete Code 200
AI Prompt 202
    .items-container 202
    .item 202
    Hover state for .item 203

| Titles inside .item (<h2>) 203

| .item-content 203

| Image inside .item 203

| Paragraph inside .item 204

| Responsive adjustments (for screens ≤ 768px): 204

| body 204

| Summary 204

Chapter 12: Detail Travel Page 205

| Main Content Display React Page 207

| Imports and Initializations 208

| Retrieve Parameters Function 209

| Fetch Content 211

| Variable Initializations 213

| Content Rendition 217

| Complete Code 223

| AI Prompt 230

| Stylesheet 232

| Root 232

| Utility Spacing 233

| Body, Heading, and Paragraph Styling 234

| List Styling 235

| Layout and Containers 236

| Image Gallery 238

| Common Blocks 239

| Section-Specific Styles 240

| Image Styling 242

| Complete Code 249

| AI Prompt 263

| Summary 264

TABLE OF CONTENTS

Chapter 13: Deployment and Future of Web Development 265

Application Deployment 265

Create Your Team and Project 265

Git Settings 266

Build and Deployment Settings 267

Environment Variables Settings 268

Environment Settings 269

Summary 270

Index 271

About the Authors

Shantanu Baruah is the President and Global Head of the Healthcare, Life Sciences, and Insurance vertical at Hexaware. He is responsible for driving global strategy, client success, and growth across the HLS vertical. His focus areas include expanding digital health capabilities, accelerating AI-led transformation, and strengthening domain-driven delivery. He brings over 25 years of experience in the healthcare and life sciences industry, with a strong track record in building high-performing global teams and leading complex client transformations. Prior to joining his current company, he served as Executive Vice President at HCLTech, where he led the Life Sciences and Healthcare business in North America. In addition to his executive roles, Shantanu is a published author of several papers and books on healthcare technology, knowledge management, digital experience, and the impact of big data on payers and providers. Shantanu is active in the app development community and has an approved app on the Apple App Store. He has been recognized as one of the top 25 Healthcare IT Executives of 2020 by the IT Services Report. Shantanu lives in New Jersey. His philanthropic outreach includes education for children in developing nations.

Nitara Baruah is a high-school sophomore at Rutgers Preparatory School. At school, she participates in Model UN and JV tennis. She was recognized by the school for achieving 50+ hours of volunteering in a single year and received an Honors Community Service Award. Highlights from her service include volunteering at ACEing Autism, where she helped children with special needs learn tennis, and Tend to a Friend. Outside of school, she completed an Inspirit AI Scholars course, a selective two-week research program that focused on the ethical issues when using an AI tool named COMPAS in the courtroom to predict a criminal's likelihood of recidivism. She implemented segments

ABOUT THE AUTHORS

of linear and logistic regression, neural networks, convolutional neural networks, and NLPs when researching this topic and demonstrated teamwork skills, understanding complex topics, and research. She also attended TARGET, a selective STEM program at Rutgers University, where she collaborated to design, model (using TinkerCAD), and build a functional canoe based on principles of buoyancy. Other projects she engineered include a reaction-time game using Python and Arduino, a battery-bearing bridge, and a miniature walking robot.

About the Technical Reviewer

With over a decade of experience in the San Francisco Bay Area, **Mohit Menghnani** is a seasoned technologist recognized for architecting and scaling robust full-stack solutions. Specializing in modern JavaScript ecosystems, React, Node.js, and GraphQL, he has successfully led cross-functional teams and delivered enterprise-grade applications across telecommunications, subscription commerce, and enterprise planning.

He is also a prolific tech writer and thought leader, regularly contributing to Forbes, DZone, and HackerNoon. In addition to technical writing, Mohit serves as a technical reviewer for multiple IEEE conferences worldwide. He also reviews books for various publications, further underscoring his dedication to advancing the field and mentoring the next generation of developers.

Acknowledgments

Writing a book on technology is a time-intensive journey – one that goes beyond putting thoughts on paper to writing code, testing it, and ensuring its completeness. I owe immense gratitude to my wife, Kapila Sood, for her unwavering support and patience as I devoted countless hours to bringing this book to life.

I am deeply grateful to my mother, Meenu Baruah, who first recognized the spark of writing in me and consistently encouraged me to nurture it.

I also wish to honor my father, Late Sailender Nath Baruah, who first introduced me to the world of software at a time when computers were far from commonplace. His early influence shaped much of the path I walk today.

Finally, I extend my heartfelt thanks to the incredible Apress team for their guidance and support in making this book a reality. Special thanks to Anandadeep Roy for her interest in this book and also for providing valuable editorial help, Shobana Srinivasan for her tireless coordination, and Mohit Menghnani for diligently reviewing my code, ensuring its accuracy, and offering insightful suggestions that strengthened the book's structure and flow.

Introduction

This book is a practical guide to modern web development leveraging generative AI tools such as ChatGPT and Perplexity. It combines the fundamentals of full-stack development – HTML, CSS, JavaScript, React, Node.js, and MongoDB – with the power of prompt engineering to make coding more accessible, faster, and more creative.

We will build a travel experience application called the Half Time Travel project (www.thehalftimewhistle.com). Through this application, you'll learn how to design, build, and deploy a content-driven web application, using AI to accelerate the development process. Some of the key aspects you will learn are

- Full-stack web application development
- Prompt engineering
- Using CDN to handle large file renditions
- React and Node.js to build front-end applications

Whether you are a beginner or an experienced developer exploring new tools or a Gen AI enthusiast, this book will help you gain the skills and confidence to create modern applications and adapt to the future of web development.

CHAPTER 1

Introduction to Modern Web Development

The Web Development Landscape

Web development has evolved quite dramatically from the earlier Web 1.0 world. While Web 1.0 had static web pages, Web 2.0 introduced the world concept of user-generated content, user interactivity with content, and general collaboration. Then came Web 3.0, which put the user in the center, making processing decentralized with concepts such as blockchain, smart contracts, and peer-to-peer networks.

From being purely information-driven static sites, the web applications today are dynamic and intelligent. Websites such as Amazon and Facebook get, on an average, anywhere between 90 and 130 million visitors per day, providing complex business functions at scale and speed. In today's web world, the amount of content that gets generated and consumed has skyrocketed, and data-driven insights add many dimensions to the consumer-centric dynamic web application that the world demands. This is further getting accentuated with the advent of artificial intelligence, for the data-driven dynamic behavior of web applications will further expand multifold.

Did you know? In around 0.05 seconds, users determine whether they stay on a website or leave. The attractiveness of your web page layout solely determines how long users will stay engaged with your information. Studies have shown that 38% of users leave a website if it looks too boring or unattractive (sweor.com).

CHAPTER 1   INTRODUCTION TO MODERN WEB DEVELOPMENT

In this ever-evolving web world, it is essential to note what options one must have to develop cutting-edge web applications. The following list summarizes some of the available options.

Static Web Applications: Static sites are easy to develop. These sites are fast, secure (using protocols such as HTTPS), and easy to maintain. Most of the static web applications are built using HTML and CSS, and traditionally, all web pages and images are stored and made available from a web server. These sites are perfect for informational sites and usually have a landing page, a collection of portfolio pages, images, and informational content. These applications are mostly one-directional and, at most, may have a web form to capture some contact information. In summary, static web applications are perfect for informational sites but are challenged when you need bi-directional behavior and data-driven insights.

Content Management Systems (CMS): Static websites are not suitable when content updates/changes frequently. In such scenarios, the Content Management Web Platform serves as an ideal solution. There are platforms such as WordPress and Wix, which are popular in the B2C segment, where users can create blogs, small business information sites, and other recreational web applications in which content changes frequently. In the B2B corporate world, there are products such as Adobe and Sitecore that allow similar functionalities but provide more complex workflows and functions to meet large corporations' needs.

CMS offers easy-to-use templates for content creation, language translation capabilities, workflow for content approval/routing, and the ability to publish pages to multiple environments. It has built-in version management, and large and complex content-driven sites can be easily managed using such platforms. All these functionalities could be achieved without writing code, as CMS relies on intuitive interfaces and pre-designed templates. These platforms, although great for product sites, can be restrictive. Some of the constraints are listed below:

- **Design Constraints**: Customization of layout and adding unique features (e.g., a custom carousel of dynamic images) are difficult.

- **Limited Dynamic Behavior**: Custom development is required for advanced database-driven features and integrations.

- **Challenges with Integration**: Integrating third-party APIs is complex and often unsupported.

- **Full-Stack Frameworks**: Full-stack frameworks provide complete freedom to design a dynamic web application, with integration to third-party APIs, leveraging the power of a persistent data layer. Full-stack frameworks are popular but complex, and mastering these frameworks requires a steep learning curve; however, with the advent of Gen AI, learning could be accelerated. Besides the learning curve, it provides greater flexibility and control to implement advanced features into your application. There are many full-stack frameworks available. Some of the most popular ones are Node.js, Next.js, and Django.

The importance of having a good web page design is crucial, as 75% of users admit to determining a company's credibility based on its website design (sweor.com).

Our book will demonstrate the use of the React Framework with MongoDB as a data layer to build a full-stack web application. We will use prompt engineering to generate most of our code/configuration and leverage the power of AI to make complex web application coding an easier endeavor.

The Rise of Generative AI and Prompt Engineering: As generative AI advances, the way we look at web development has dramatically transformed. Platforms, like Perplexity, change how users approach web development and leverage prompt engineering to build complex web applications with agility and speed. While Gen AI and prompt engineering have made it more accessible than ever for users, however, to create robust web applications, a deeper appreciation of core design principles and a greater depth in writing prompts is required for success. Large language models (LLMs) can only answer intelligently when the question asked (read as a prompt) is well designed. Moreover, it is also important to note that code generated by large language models should be thoroughly analyzed and understood before deploying to production, as the LLM sometimes hallucinates and may result in buggy, functionally incorrect, and vulnerable code in the environment. This book is designed to help you learn such skills that will help you create advanced web applications with ease and confidence.

Security Considerations: As we will learn to develop complex web applications, it is critical to keep security considerations front and center, particularly when web applications will be available for a broad audience. Some of the key considerations are

- Encrypting sensitive data during transmission (HTTPS) and at rest.
- Authentication and access control for a web application that has user-based content access.
- Protecting against session hijacking by securely managing sessions across users.
- Using secure coding practices – avoid SQL injection, security testing, and variable usage.
- Using the right and most stable version of the underlying software. Software updates address vulnerabilities.

Who Is This Book For?

This book is for individuals with a curious mind and who are interested in learning coding through prompt engineering using generative AI platforms, like Perplexity. This book is for individuals of all ages and coding levels – whether you are a student, teacher, adult, or motivated coder aspiring to be a professional. This book could help you accelerate your learning curve.

Although no prior coding experience is needed, an appreciation of general coding principles, understanding of web development architecture, and a good knowledge of design frameworks could immensely help in grasping the concepts faster. The chapters are designed to first make you understand the fundamentals and then guide you through the process of coding details using the power of prompt engineering. Our goal is to help you gain complete confidence in building a fully functional web application, and as you will come to the end of this book, you will gain skillsets for not only building a web application but also learn the art of prompt engineering.

How the Book Is Structured

Getting Started

The first section of our book is to get you acquainted with the toolset that we will use to develop our web application. It has the following two sections:

- **Introduction**: Provides an overview of web development paradigms, different avenues to develop web applications, and the concept of Gen AI-based prompt engineering.

- **Environment Setup**: This section will detail out all the tools that you will need to build a full-stack web application. We will use CLT as our command-line interface, VS Code as our IDE, GitHub as our code repository, MongoDB to persist our application data, and Vercel as our web server. For demonstration purposes, we will use the free version of each of the product. The section will provide the tool overview, setup instructions, and any configuration elements required to get your environment ready for coding.

Web Development Foundations

This section will provide you with a solid foundation for full-stack development and will walk through the foundational details of HTML, CSS, JavaScript, front-end frameworks (React), and back-end technologies (MongoDB). Furthermore, this section will explore web protocols and architectures so that, by the end of this section, you have a deep appreciation and expanded knowledge of full-stack development. The following are some of the important sections:

- **Core Concepts**: Cover detailed concepts of HTML 5.0, CSS 3.0, core JavaScript, front-end frameworks, back-end technologies, web protocols, and architecture.

- **Front-End Frameworks**: Everything that you need to render a responsive design web application is covered in this section. React. js framework, advanced HTML, CSS, JavaScript fundamentals, SPA design, state management, and responsive design are the core parts of this section.

- **Back End and Database**: Data persistence is key to any dynamic, complex web application. In this section, we will focus on the toolset MongoDB, data modeling, query optimization, and data persistence. We will also learn how to securely access content from back-end repositories to display on the front end.

AI and Prompt Engineering in Practice

This section will introduce you to practical techniques that you can use to generate your code in an accelerated manner. We will also explore concepts of code debugging and code optimization for creating a scalable web application. The concept of good prompt engineering will be explored deeply. The following are some of the key sections:

- **Generative AI in Web Development Applications**: This includes prompt engineering techniques, AI-assisted coding and debugging, and front-end web design features.
- **Experience Design**: In this section, you can learn about site design, navigation, form-factor consideration, and faster image display and orientation.

Building the Full-Stack Application

This book is designed for you to learn how to build a dynamic website. The site is already available (www.thehalftimewhistle.com). This is our family's personal site on our travel experiences. As you go through this section, you will learn every aspect of building this web application from scratch. This section will lead you through the process of building the project by dissecting the code, exploring its ideas, and demonstrating how pieces of the code come together to provide the end functionality. The following are some of the key sections:

- **Project Setup**: How to set up the project environment
- **Code Walkthrough**: Step-by-step explanation of the entire code, which includes front-end interface, server integration, dynamic content retrieval, and consideration of core design elements

- **Component Architecture**: Highlights how parts of the code work together, including concepts about accessibility and responsive design

Deployment and Optimization

After the application is complete and functional, it is important to market it in the best way possible to share it with the world. For this to be done, you need to ensure your site is configured right, can scale for high-speed, secure, and accessible across all devices. This helps with a positive user experience, which is vital for your web application's success and growth. The following are some of the key sections:

- **Full-Stack Integration**: Connecting front end and back end to deliver a seamless experience.

- **Deployment Strategies**: Providing details on Vercel (our deployment provider). Integrating VS Code to GitHub and GitHub to Vercel for incremental deployment planning.

- **Performance and Responsiveness**: Techniques to optimize both front-end and back-end code, asset handling, and Vercel's interactive elements for Observability monitoring and tuning. While we will use Vercel's built-in Observability stack to get the visibility of the system, it is important to note that there are other Observability players such as Datadog, Open Telemetry, and Splunk that offer comprehensive visibility for highly reliable application infrastructure.

The Future of Web Development

This is the final section of the book, with its aim of inspiring individuals to be lifelong learners, as the role of AI is always growing. This section will explore the web development world today and how to be successful in a world that is changing rapidly. Some key sections are listed below:

- **Emerging Technologies**: This section will provide our view on where web development and prompt engineering are headed and the role of applications built on top of a Gen AI platform.

- **AI Trends**: AI is changing at lightning speed. New models are now released on a monthly basis. This section provides our perspective on how to keep abreast with the ever-changing world of AI.

- **Career Growth**: This section provides you with tools and thoughts on what one can do to ensure they can make a rewarding career leveraging AI.

Introducing Half Time Whistle

This book will use a real-world example to help individuals connect their reading to a website that has already been made. The website is called the Half Time Whistle (www.thehalftimewhistle.com), which is a personal travel site that shares our family's travel adventures. The website includes the following elements:

- Organizing our travel experiences by continent. Each continent has regions where we have traveled.

- Every region will have a collection of travel itineraries or places.

- Each of the travel itineraries will have details on the place, our experience, interesting facts about the place, a collection of photos, and valuable tips.

- Every itinerary can have sub-itineraries as well.

- The site ensures you can reach any content in less than four clicks.

- There are curated sections for users to consume as well – for example, a 12-day trip to Japan or hiking trails in California.

Using the Half Time Whistle Project as a guide, we will help you understand concepts of generative AI, prompt engineering, and full-stack development. You will also learn how to put together a complex set of tools for full-stack development. Happy learning.

Why Learn with Prompt Engineering?

This book can be used as a standalone book to learn full-stack coding using React.js. Although the site must be architected and designed, the code is generated using Gen AI. There are many benefits of using prompt engineering. Some of them are listed below:

- **Low Entry Barrier**: Any age or level can begin building, including those with minimal coding experience.

- **Accelerated Learning**: Instant feedback, explanations, examples, and thoughts are provided through AI platforms, which help with mastering hard concepts quickly.

- **Innovation and Experimentation**: Instills curiosity as prompt engineering helps individuals experience new ideas and technologies.

- **Career Growth**: Helps tremendously with career growth as AI is rapidly changing and becoming more integral to software development. Being able to know and understand AI is a useful skill today.

- **Speed to Market**: The agility and speed that prompt engineering can give you is unparalleled. This entire website, from concept to build, was done in less than three weeks.

What's Next?

Get ready to start your journey through each stage of the design, development, and deployment process. Using this book, you will sharpen your skillset, expand your knowledge, and use the Half Time Whistle Project, prompt engineering, and generative AI to make your web application with confidence and control.

Summary

This chapter provided an overview of the paradigms of web technologies and how Gen AI is weighing into it. It further explained the benefit of prompt engineering and provided a comprehensive view of how the book is laid out. The book uses an example (a live web application `www.thehalftimewhistle.com`) to explain the concepts and provides an overview of the site, and the approach is also provided for users to understand and appreciate.

CHAPTER 2

Environment Setup

Introduction

In this chapter, we will learn how to set up our environment to build our example web application. We will go through the tools needed and the list of steps we need to execute for setting up our development environment. Please note that most tools need to be downloaded to your local machine. For the remaining, we will configure in the remote environment provided by the software vendor.

Prerequisite

We are going to set our web application environment on macOS. The instructions given below assume you have a MacBook Pro with preferably 2.6 GHz 6-core Intel Core i7 processor with 6 GB of 2400 MHz DDR4 memory and about 50GB of free hard disk space. Also, install the latest macOS version. As we are writing this document, the current macOS version is Sequoia 15.0.

Install Xcode CLT

Xcode Command Line Terminal is a critical interface to execute important configuration- and operation-related commands. We will use CLT to install Node.js, configure the Git repository, perform cleanup activities, and perform GIT operations.

You need to install the XCODE CLT to get access to the Xcode command-line interface. Follow the steps to get this setup for your development environment:

CHAPTER 2   ENVIRONMENT SETUP

- For installing CLT (and other packages), you need to install Homebrew. You can download the package from the following URL:

  https://github.com/Homebrew/brew/releases/tag/4.3.22

- After installing Homebrew, open the Terminal window and execute the following command:

  brew update

- You can also install CLT by running the following command:

  xcode-select –install

You can use either method to install the CLT (Homebrew or xcode-select-install).

Install Git

To make our application Git-aware, we need to install Git. Installing Git makes sure functionalities such as version control, log, differential push, and push history are stored in the local environment. Follow the following steps to install Git:

- Change directory to the path where your project is, for example:

  cd /projects/thehalftimewhistle

- Initialize a new Git repository:

  git init

- Add all your files to the new repository:

  git add .

- Since we have a remote GitHub repository, we need to connect to the same one. The URL below you can get by logging into your GitHub repository and clicking Code, as shown below, and then executing the command below:

  git remote add origin <remote-repository-URL>

CHAPTER 2 ENVIRONMENT SETUP

Did you know? GitHub supports over 300 million repositories, some of which have unexpected uses! Although this platform is mostly used for coding, musicians and writers also use GitHub to share sheet music and stories.

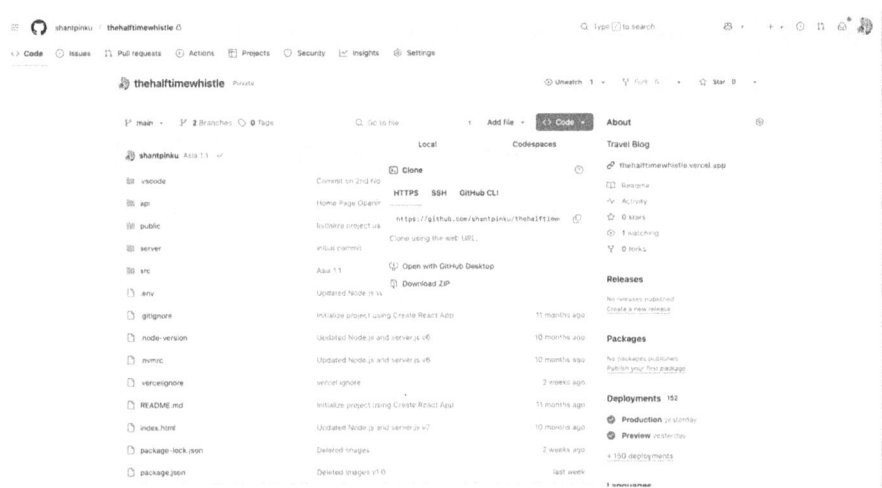

Install VS Code

VS Code is the IDE interface where we will define our project and use it for writing and debugging our code.

We are going to use Visual Studio as our IDE for developing our web application. Follow along the steps to set up VS Code:

- Download the VS Code install from the following URL:

    https://code.visualstudio.com/docs/?dv=osx

- Once VS Code is installed, open the IDE and locate the Extension icon on the left and search for "Live Server". "Live Server" allows you to create a local development environment.

CHAPTER 2   ENVIRONMENT SETUP

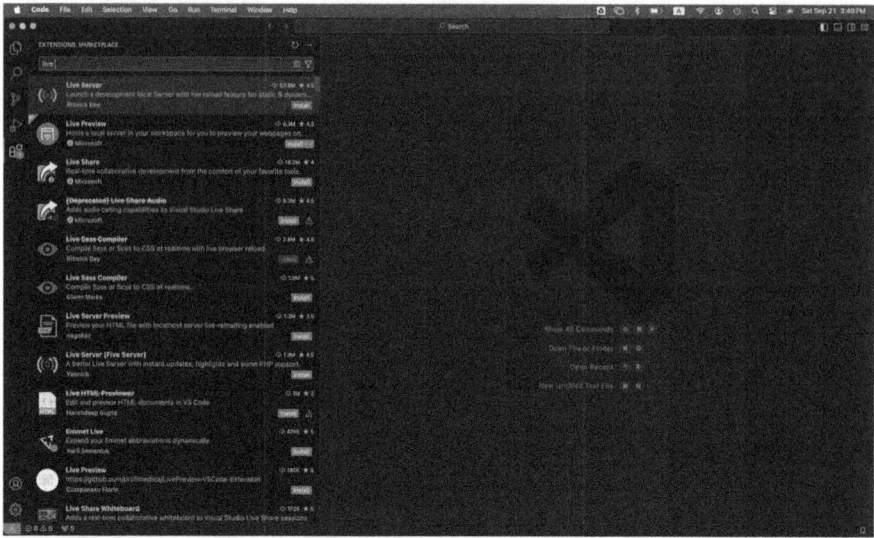

Once found, install the extension.

- We will store all our code in GitHub. This will help us to have multiple users code as a team. To enable GitHub integration, install the **"GitHub Pull Requests and Issues"**.

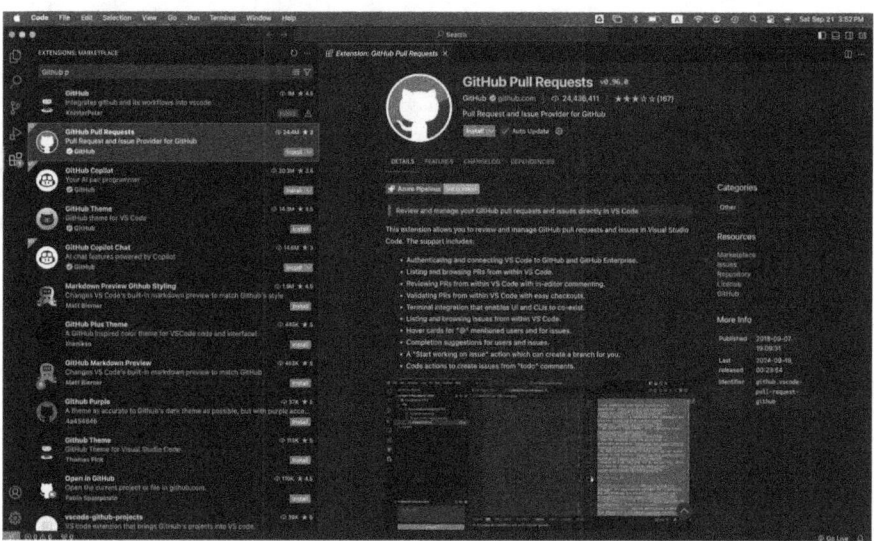

CHAPTER 2   ENVIRONMENT SETUP

- Finally, configure for autosave. Search for autosave and set it to "onFocusChange". This will enable automatic saving.

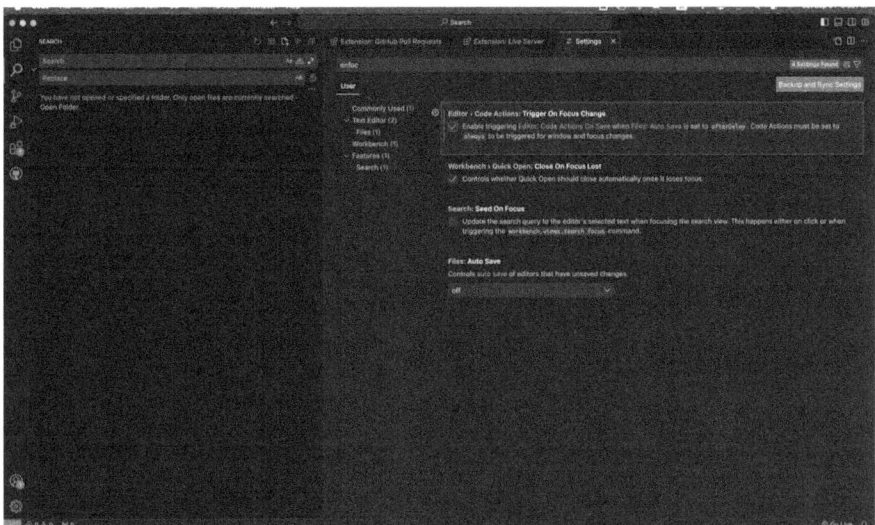

Setting Up GitHub

GitHub is our code repository. In GitHub, you can make your code public for others to contribute to or reuse. Our repository will be private.

We need to have a GitHub account to ensure we can leverage GitHub as a code repository for our travel web application. Follow the steps mentioned below.

Creation of GitHub Repository

- Open a web browser and open the URL www.github.com.
- Create a new account (if you have an account, then log in to your account).
- Click **"New Repository"** and create a new repository for our web application (give any name).

CHAPTER 2   ENVIRONMENT SETUP

- Make your repository private (if you make it public, the code will be available to the entire community).

- Before creating the repository, make sure you don't initialize with a README.

- Create the repository.

Create a Project Directory

- From the Finder window, go to your user folder and create the project folder for your project and under that your "project name".

    Example: /Users/<user name>/projects/<Your Project Name>

Setting Up VS Code to Store Source Code in GitHub

- Launch Visual Studio on your computer.

- Open the terminal in VS Code. You can find Terminal under the View menu option. You can also open Terminal directly from the Terminal menu and select the "New Terminal" option.

- Change the directory to your project folder using the command below. By default, you should be in your user folder:

    ```
    cd projects/<Your Project Name>
    ```

CHAPTER 2   ENVIRONMENT SETUP

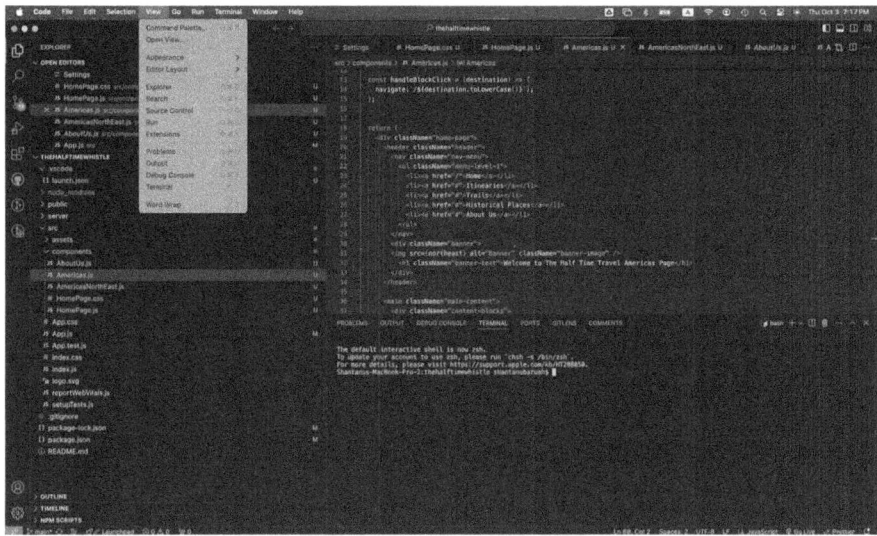

- Go to Visual Code and open the project folder by going to File ➤ Open Folder and navigating to the project folder on your local drive.

- The next step is to clone the GitHub repository from our local drive to the GitHub cloud. Type the following command in the Terminal window:

  git clone https://github.com/yourusername/your-repo-name.git

  Replace "yourusername" and "your-repo-name" with your actual GitHub username and repository name.

- VS Code should automatically now detect the GitHub repository. Click the Source Control icon in the left sidebar (it looks like a branch).

CHAPTER 2   ENVIRONMENT SETUP

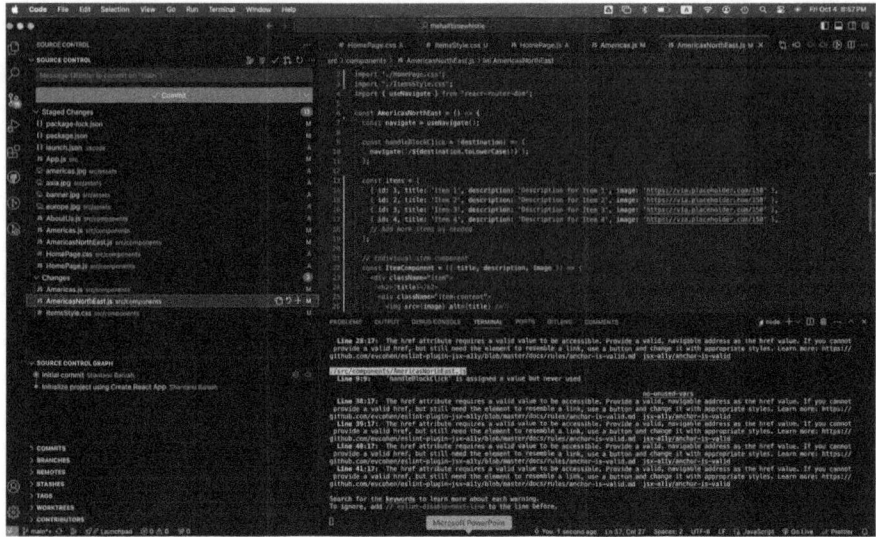

- At last, you can verify on GitHub by logging in to your account and checking the repository.

MongoDB Setup

MongoDB is the most well-known NoSQL database in the world!

MongoDB is our data persistence layer. All the information related to the places the user has visited will be stored in a MongoDB database. We will use the MongoDB API to query the records to be displayed on our web application.

The final stage of our configuration is setting up the database for persisting data for our web application. You can set up MongoDB using the CLT or directly use the MongoDB web application. We will show you both the methods in the section below.

CHAPTER 2   ENVIRONMENT SETUP

Setting Up MongoDB Using the MongoDB Web Interface

- Open a web browser and type the following URL. You will see the following screen:

  `https://www.mongodb.com`

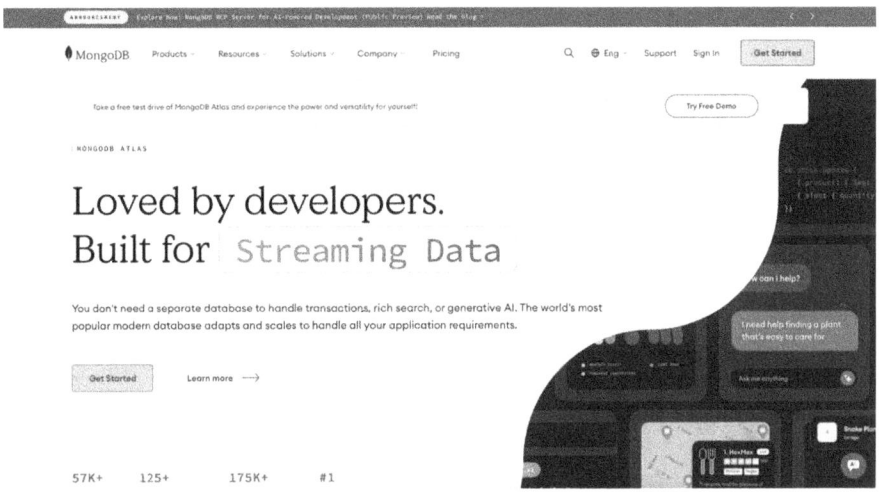

- Create a user profile using the **Get Started** option. You can also use OAuth to create a profile using a Google or GitHub profile. I am logging in using my Google account. Once logged in, you will see a screen like this.

CHAPTER 2   ENVIRONMENT SETUP

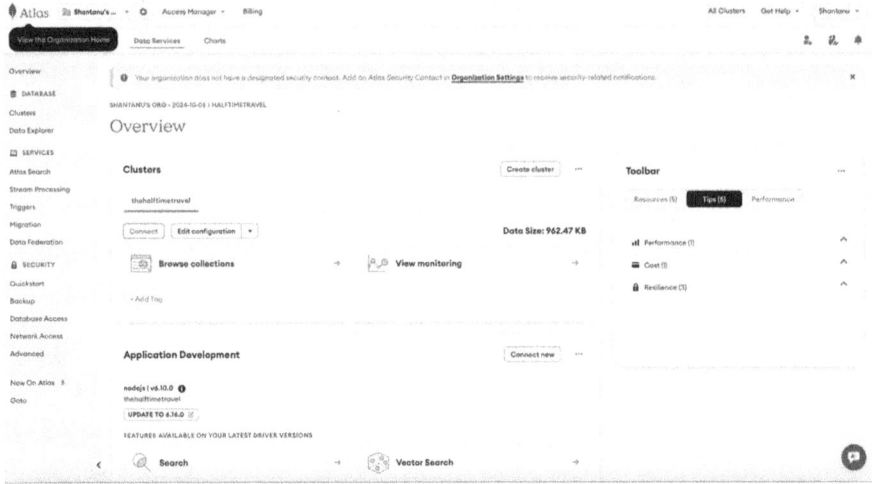

- Please note that, although MongoDB is a paid service, there is a free option with limited capabilities available for beginners to explore. You can always upgrade to a dedicated or a flex model later.

- Next, you need to create a project and a cluster for your application. Cluster will hold all collections (tables) that will store all relevant data for your web application. Our cluster name is **thehalftimetravel.** You need to make sure your cluster name is unique. The screen below shows the cluster name of our web application.

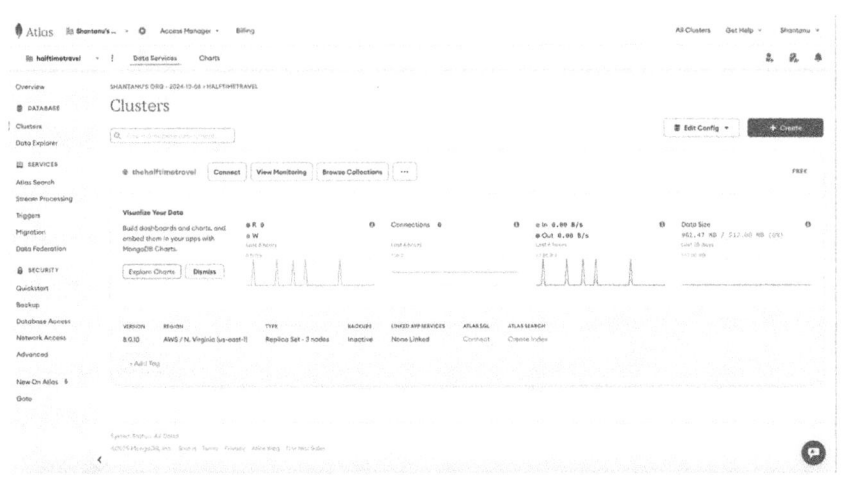

CHAPTER 2 ENVIRONMENT SETUP

- Click the Browse Collection, and it will take you to the Data Explorer screen. In this screen, you can create any number of databases. A database has a collection of tables. Our database name is placesDB.

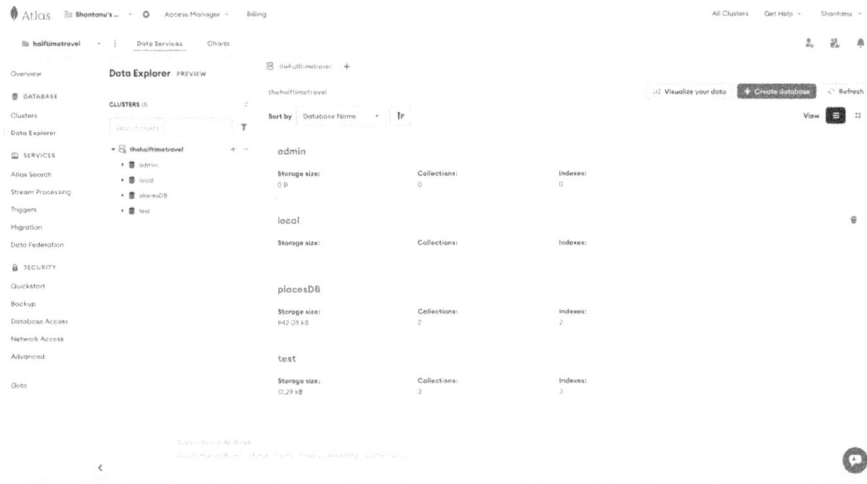

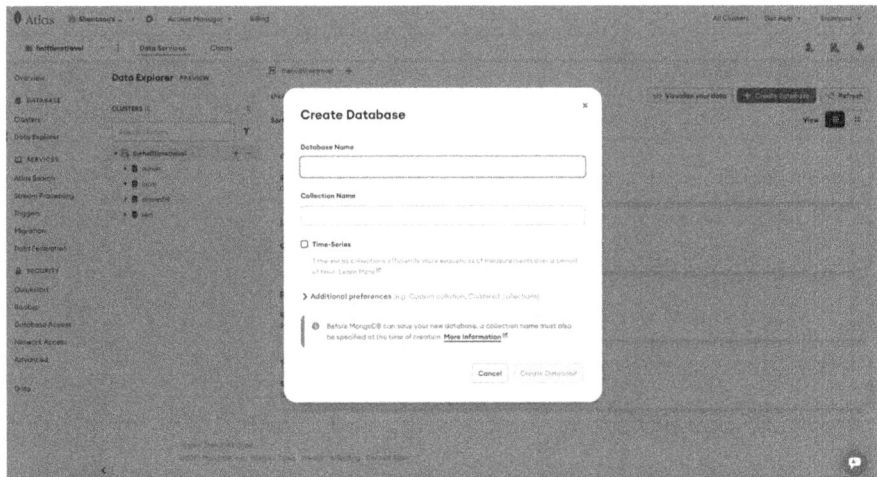

- MongoDB database stores data as collections and documents instead of traditional relational database tables and rows. There are three main concepts in MongoDB for file records:

21

- **Document**: Document is the information you want to store at the record level. The values are stored in a field/value pair combination, and every document can have its own structure. This format is called BSON (Binary JSON).
- **Collection**: A group of documents is called a collection. We have two collections in our application, as described below:
  - **places**: This table contains details of all places in a particular region.
  - **placedetails**: One place can have many different attractions. This table captures details of each of the attractions of a place in the **places** table.
- **Database**: A physical container of collection is called a database.

Creating MongoDB Using Terminal and Homebrew

You can create a MongoDB project, cluster, databases, and collections using the command-line interface. The steps below provide a quick guide to achieve the same:

- Open your command-line interface on your Mac and execute the following command. Please note that the MongoDB version can be changed based on the current version:

  ```bash
  brew tap mongodb/brew
  brew update
  brew install mongodb-community@7.0
  ```

- Next, we will establish MongoDB to start as a service so that it comes up as a macOS service. Execute the following command to achieve the same:

  ```bash
  brew services start mongodb-community@7.0
  ```

If you ever need to pause the running MongoDB service, you could issue the following command:

```bash
brew services stop mongodb-community@7.0
```

Summary

In this chapter, we learned how to set up the environment to develop our web application. We installed the terminal and set up VS Code for code development, GitHub as our code repository, and MongoDB for data persistence. In the next chapter, we will learn all about front-end development, the bedrock of why we develop web applications.

CHAPTER 3

Foundations of Modern Web Development

Introduction

The digital age has transformed the way the internet shares, consumes, and utilizes information. Websites are no longer only pieces of text and images, which connect individuals and their ideas across the world. They are now dynamic, interactive, and complex web applications handling millions of users and transactions at lightning speed.

This chapter explains the Half Time Whistle web application (`https://www.thehalftimewhistle.com`), the website that will help you learn the basics of web development. We will go through the rationale behind the technology stack we chose, the architectural decisions, and the power of the modern full-stack development approach. We will also delve into the reasoning behind building a custom website instead of relying on website builders like WordPress or Wix.

The Vision Behind the Half Time Whistle

"We love to travel as a family – exploring new destinations, experiencing diverse cultures, and embracing the life of true wanderers. When we plan a trip, the process of creating the itinerary is often a daunting task. We prefer to explore like locals – renting cars, staying in Airbnbs, and stepping off the beaten path.

For a long time, we wanted to create a log of all our travel experiences in one place – a space that not only serves as our family travelogue, allowing us to relive our cherished memories, but also as a resource for others. We hope that people will read about our adventures and, perhaps, feel inspired to visit some of the places we've been.

CHAPTER 3   FOUNDATIONS OF MODERN WEB DEVELOPMENT

Why the name "Half Time Whistle"?

In any game, a whistle signals a break – a time to refuel, rejuvenate, and rethink. Our Half Time Whistle website is inspired by this concept, encouraging you to take a pause from your busy life to wander, explore, and rediscover the world.

Half Time Whistle is not just a travel website; it's a piece of our heart and soul. It's a collection of our memories, woven together with passion and love. We hope you enjoy this space as much as we enjoy creating and nurturing it."

What you read above are the true sentiments that went behind building this site. We knew that the way we desired to curate content, provide an intuitive interface, and organize travel experience, none of the commercially available platforms could meet it; hence, we decided to custom-build the website using full-stack technology. The goal was to develop a website that was high-speed, visually appealing, and customizable for future growth. For this to be achieved, several technologies were chosen:

- **React.js**: As our core front-end technology platform, supported by an ecosystem of tools such as Node.js, npm, and webpack to build an intuitive, interactive, scalable, and visually appealing web experience.

- **Visual Studio Code (VS Code)**: This is our main IDE (interactive design environment). VS Code was integrated with GitHub for code version management and Vercel for code deployment.

- **GitHub**: As the code repository. The code repository is currently marked as private. We are currently using the free version.

- **Vercel**: For web hosting. We are currently using the free version (for a personal project).

- **MongoDB**: For data persistence. MongoDB stores data as JSON objects. Note, although MongoDB can store images and blobs, in our application, we will store them in GitHub Pages CDN environment; this helps in faster rendition of images, enhancing user experience.

- **Generative AI**: We will use generative AI to achieve most of the code development. We will use Perplexity and ChatGPT for most of the code generation. Please note that with vibe coding, you can generate code from EPIC and stories directly. This book does not explain the use of those technologies.

These were the core technologies used. In the subsequent chapters, we will learn the role of each of the tech stacks in detail.

Choosing the right technologies for your website is more important than you think. The technology you use to build your website impacts its run speed and how collaborative it can be – the wrong technology can be detrimental to your website's progress and cause it to lag behind.

Choosing the wrong technology at the start makes it more difficult to change it later as well. Think of the technology you use as the spine of your project – if something within it malfunctions, it ultimately makes it harder for it to support the body of your website.

Web Development Fundamentals
Web Basics and Core Technologies

The three main pillars, or core technologies, of every website include HTML, CSS, and JavaScript. A description of each pillar is given below:

- **HTML (Hypertext Markup Language)**: We will use HTML5 for building our website. HTML5 is a markup language that provides a DOM (Document Object Model) structure for building websites. It has a collection of built-in components that we will leverage to build the front end of our web application. Most of our HTML code will be embedded as part of React code. This seamless integration of code not only enhances code readability but also increases the maintainability of the application.

- **CSS (Cascading Style Sheets)**: We will use CSS 3.0 for organizing the visual layout for our website. Besides the color, font, style, and layout, CSS also helps to create responsive design pages. Responsive design helps in rendering the page automatically based on the form factor of a device, allowing the web application to adjust based on the platform or environment where the website is viewed.

- **JavaScript**: JavaScript is a front-end code language that helps to control the dynamic behavior on web pages. JavaScript makes the web page most interactive, including elements such as real-time data updates, asynchronous server requests, and animations. We will use React.js, which is a JavaScript framework, to build our web application. JavaScript provides the concept of components as the building blocks of UI elements. These are reusable components that bring a great deal of modularity and use JSX to describe what the interface should look like in a declarative way. Together, JavaScript, React components, and JSX provide a structured and efficient approach to creating an interactive, scalable, and maintainable web application.

Working together in harmony, these technologies help create a strong, interactive, and complex web application.

Understanding HTML, CSS, and JavaScript

Now that we have defined the core technologies, let us learn in this section how they interact with each other to create complex web applications.

- **HTML (Hypertext Markup Language)**: The "backbone of a website" as it organizes the content and its elements. It also allows browsers to display and interpret the information on the web page. The web browser has the HTML DOM object, which it manipulates based on user interaction to deliver an interactive data display.

- **CSS (Cascading Stylesheets)**: Takes the dull web page and transforms it into a visually appealing website to ensure it looks good. Its responsive design helps to maintain the aesthetics of the page across all browsers, form factors, and devices.

- **JavaScript**: Acts like the brain of your application as it makes the web page dynamic by applying control logic, accepting and interpreting user interactions, and asynchronous data communication to back-end servers.

Frameworks, such as React.js, then go on to build on top of these technologies and help transform the web application into more complex interfaces that are secure, scalable, and easy to manage.

Web Protocols and Architectures

Web pages depend on different architectures and protocols to function seamlessly across browsers and devices. These include

- **HTTP (Hypertext Transfer Protocol)**: HTTP is the foundation for transforming information across different devices as it controls the format of messages and how they are transmitted across servers. There is the HTTPS (S stands for secure) protocol as well, which helps data exchange securely by applying encryption technology. This is a must for all web applications to prevent hackers and rogue agents from stealing user data (e.g., credit card information and personal data).

- **TCP/IP (Transmission Control Protocol/Internet Protocol)**: Secure transfer of data packets across the internet and back-end servers.

Appreciating and understanding these protocols are must to ensure your web application is using some of the best security standards and certificates for the reliable transfer of data and information.

Introduction to Front-End and Back-End Concepts

Web development is typically divided into two main domains:

- **Front-End Development**: Front-end development centers user interface and consists of what the users interact with and see. This includes HTML, CSS, and JavaScript and different JavaScript frameworks such as React.js.

- **Back-End Development**: Comprises what drives the web application. This includes databases, authentication protocols, and APIs (Application Programming Interface). Examples of back-end technologies include APIs, Python, and MongoDB.

CHAPTER 3   FOUNDATIONS OF MODERN WEB DEVELOPMENT

To become a proficient full-stack developer, appreciating and learning both the front-end and back-end concepts is necessary.

Why Full-Stack Development over WordPress or Wix?

WordPress, Wix, and other website builders have made creating simple websites easier than ever, as they offer templates, plug-ins, and other built-in features to launch a website with very minimal coding knowledge. Since they are templatized and are designed to work for the masses, they come with limitations:

- **Limits on Customization**: Templates, though on the outside seem convenient, aren't as restrictive as they impede creativity on how you want to lay out your page and branding.

- **Performance**: While plug-ins are a great way to enhance a website's functionality (there are 1000s of them available, both paid and free versions), they can become difficult to manage, particularly when your website grows. To scale and handle users, you will need to resort to more expensive alternatives or often resort to other options.

- **Limits on Control**: Challenges with optimizing performance arise as the website builders limit access to source code and server configurations. This also makes it challenging for enhanced security and integration among other systems.

- **Routing Challenges**: Tools like WordPress and Wix have limitations on flex routing. Although these applications provide plug-ins for some limited routing capabilities, moving between pages, API calls, and dynamic URL creation and routing is largely not possible.

On the contrary, full-stack development offers a multitude of flexibility as outlined below:

- **Control**: You will have complete control of every aspect of the website. This ranges from design to how it functions and can be tailored to your specific needs.

- **Scalability**: Frameworks and cloud platforms (like Vercel) make it easier to scale applications based on user growth.

- **Optimized Performance**: You can optimize performance by implementing concepts like Single-Page Architecture (SPA) or creating an asynchronous data request protocol, providing a positive user experience.

- **Future-Proof**: Technology is always progressing; full-stack solutions adapt to this evolving technology and integrate new and different features without the constraint of a platform limitation.

These advantages are beneficial for web applications like the Half Time Whistle, as they allow the website to continuously evolve, grow, scale, and deliver a productive experience to users.

Summary

Designing a full-stack web application provides the flexibility that a modern-day web application demands. Today's web applications demand complex functions with scalable, secure, and evolving design principles. This chapter provided an overview of core technologies, web protocols, and architectures that can be leveraged to meet such evolving demand.

The chapter also explored the importance of front-end and back-end development, leveraging technologies such as React.js, VS Code, Gen AI, and MongoDB. We also discussed the Half Time Whistle's vision, defined key considerations on its development principles, and discussed why full-stack development is a great option for complex website development.

In the next section, we will dig deeper into each individual technology and explore how they work together to make a functioning web application.

CHAPTER 4

Front-End Development

Introduction

While there are many factors that determine the difference between a successful web application and an unsuccessful one, the prominent among all is the interface. How intuitive your website is, the image layout, responsiveness, and form factors – all of these are directly related to front-end development of your web application. Front end is as much art as it is science. It is where the code meets your user base and always remains as a keystone character that determines whether your site will be liked by the masses or will dissolve into oblivion.

In this chapter, we will explore all the fundamentals of front-end design, most of which you will see in the subsequent chapters in action as we build our example website. We will explore concepts such as HTML5 – building blocks of user interface – CSS framework to artistically display the content for user consumption, responsive design principles, JavaScript for front-end content manipulations, and the concept of single-page application design.

These concepts are the bedrock of any web application and are pivotal for creating a dynamic, engaging web application for the masses.

HTML5 Advanced Techniques

HTML has a long history of evolution from the early days of HTML 1.0 to the current version of HTML5. The user demand for complex web needs has encouraged W3C to enhance the markup language to include rich, diverse, and intuitive features. Some of the key features of HTML5 empower web developers to add features beyond mere content structuring. Some of the key features are listed below:

- Allowing users to dynamically edit content right on the browser without any additional plugins for basic in-page editing using built-in features like **contenteditable**. This helps in real-time content manipulation in a shared and open environment setup. For advanced content editing and collaboration, additional plugins and extensions would be required.

- HTML5 provides super sleek, advanced forms that enable users to add content with ease and accuracy. For example, Date Carousel, placeholder text, validation of numbers, and population of content such as address.

- Seamlessly drag and drop files from the user's machine to the browser, making file upload an easy and user-intuitive feature.

- Built-in support for video, audio, and the ability to draw graphics without the use of any third-party libraries or plugins.

- Auto detection of browser support for progressive degradation of features instead of throwing errors.

- Semantic element detection and generation for better SEO management.

- Providing offline capabilities so that the web pages can render even when the user is offline. This is supported through Progressive Web Apps (PWAs).

- Ability to get the user's geo location (with adequate user permission), allowing the application to be user-aware to render content based on user needs.

These features and more truly enable users to create powerful web applications without compromising on usability functions.

Did you know? The first web page made with HTML was created by Tim Berners-Lee in 1991.

CSS Frameworks and Responsive Design

While HTML5 provides the framework to represent content in a dynamic, responsive, and intuitive way, CSS provides the essential elements to elevate the design. Essentially, CSS controls the presentation and style, or more famously known as "skin" of your website. The following are some of the key elements that CSS offers to a web enthusiast:

- CSS helps in HTML styling, for example, while HTML5 can show a header, footer, label, text, and image – CSS helps in styling them with color, font, size, background, border, margins, layout, and positioning.

- CSS also offers animation and transition features, which can make content more intuitive and dynamic.

- The best-kept secret of CSS is the separation of content (HTML) from presentation (CSS). The same content with different CSS can have a completely different layout and presentation, which not only helps in code maintainability but also helps to keep the code clean.

- CSS styling promotes responsive design, helping you to create responsive websites. This helps in auto-form factor management, enabling content to render based on the device used.

- CSS also helps in managing accessibility standards and compliance by managing aspects such as font size, color, and styles that promote inclusion for individuals with disabilities.

- CSS helps with caching websites and images, helping to load the sites faster on websites.

When implementing CSS, there are some best practices one should follow. Some of the best practices to follow are

- Modern CSS frameworks include built-in support for accessibility (a11y) features. Some examples are automated ARIA attributes, keyboard navigation, and focus management. These techniques immensely help make the components accessible to screen reader users and also to users who are navigating using a keyboard. To enhance web accessibility, developers should follow WCAG 2.2 standards and implement such standards.

CHAPTER 4   FRONT-END DEVELOPMENT

- Implement CSS modular practices for enhancing reusability, scalability, and maintainability. A few modular principles are Block Element Modifier (BEM) and a utility-first framework such as Tailwind.

- CSS usually has the notoriety to create naming conflicts, so it is imperative to scope them to specific components and features.

Over time, there have been many CSS frameworks that have emerged that provide a built-in blueprint for developing world-class web applications. One of the most widely used CSS frameworks is Bootstrap, which has a mobile-first approach that ensures websites are responsive from the word go. The framework has pre-built components and a series of utility classes that accelerate the entire development cycle. A CSS framework typically offers the following elements:

- A flexible grid system that helps organize content in rows and columns. This helps in achieving responsive design.

- Predefined and pre-built-in styles for common UI elements.

- Predefined UI components. UI components are a collection of UI objects that perform a particular function. For example, a drop-down menu or an image carousel.

- Reset style sheets to ensure the default style sheet doesn't take over as users switch between devices and browsers.

You will see a detailed CSS layout and template for our web application, where we will leverage similar features to achieve our end goal – responsive design, easy to maintain, and device-independent designs.

CSS was also made alongside Tim Berners-Lee. It was designed by Håkon Wium Lie at CERN. Today, although CSS is mainly used for web pages, it can also be used in emails, mobile apps, and print media.

JavaScript Fundamentals

A full-stack development framework won't be complete without the mention of the scripting language JavaScript. JavaScript allows the HTML code to dynamically render content and design layout based on the user's actions, needs, and context. JavaScript provides a multitude of functionalities, and mastering them is quintessential to mastering the front-end development paradigms. Some of the key concepts that JavaScript has are listed below:

- A wide range of data types is supported by JavaScript to handle strings, numbers, Booleans, and array objects. These data types could be stored in a transient variable, which allows data manipulation capabilities for front-end developers to enhance the functionalities of their websites.

- Like any computer language, JavaScript offers simple to complex operators and operations to perform calculations, data comparison, and logical operations. These concept helps front-end developers to render content based on criteria and conditions.

- JavaScript also offers control structures and loops to make conditional branching or iterate through objects to make conditional manipulation of data elements.

- If a block of code needs to be called multiple times across code, JavaScript offers a modular design using functions.

- JavaScript also allows access to the entire page as a DOM object. Web developers can iterate through the DOM and dynamically alter it to change page behavior, giving high power to developers to control their page functions and layouts.

ECMAScript 2016 introduced significant improvements to JavaScript that make code cleaner, more readable, and efficient. Some of the key benefits are

- Availability of Arrow functions, which offer concise syntax, and lexical scoping, which simplifies callbacks and functional programming patterns.

CHAPTER 4   FRONT-END DEVELOPMENT

- Availability of Deconstruction for easy extraction of values from arrays or objects. This also helps in reducing code verbosity and provides greater clarity.

- Providing block scoping for safer variable declarations.

JavaScript provides unprecedented flexibility to front-end developers to design web applications to meet complex business needs. HTML, CSS, and JavaScript are fundamental skills a web developer should possess to create robust and scalable web applications.

React.js Framework

React.js is one of the most used front-end technologies, with a staggering 82% of JavaScript developers using it. According to a Stack Overflow report, React has a 40% popularity stat.

The web application we are going to build in this book leverages the JavaScript framework React.js. This section provides details of the framework so that you can make yourself acquainted with it before applying your learnings to build your website. React.js (often referred to as React) roots go back to Facebook (now Meta), which initially developed it and is now maintained by a large community of developers across the world. It offers a strong framework for building user interfaces that are sleek and meet the demands of the rapidly evolving complex web design needs. Today, React is one of the most popular frameworks used by many complex web platforms, some of which are mentioned below:

- Social media platforms such as Facebook and Instagram
- Streaming services such as Netflix and BBC
- Complex web commerce sites such as Shopify and Walmart
- Popular sites such as Airbnb and *The New York Times*

The following are some of the key features that you should be aware of before using React as a framework for your web application:

- React manages the entire component life cycle from creation to destruction. This helps it to optimize the DOM for performance.

- React also offers built-in functions to manage state. This helps to sustain information at the user interface level across screens and pages.

- React interestingly manages a virtual DOM, which is a lightweight DOM of the actual DOM, updating only the parts needed. This drastically improves the application response time.

- React offers a unique diffing algorithm that re-renders the pages, determining what minimal changes are required. The user experience is a lot smoother, and performance is top-notch because of this diffing algorithm.

To summarize, React has the following key building blocks that make it one of the most popular web development languages in the world:

- **Component-Based Architecture**: Modular components that are self-contained. This makes the code more reusable, maintainable, and scalable.

- **Virtual DOM**: A lightweight Document Object Model that is separate from the browser DOM. This allows React to update only the necessary changes, making the application lighter and speedier.

- **JSX**: React JavaScript XML allows users to write HTML-like code directly within JavaScript, making it super easy to create and manage components.

- **Unidirectional Data Flow**: In React, data can only flow in one direction from a parent component to a child component. This helps in data and state management easily.

- **React Native**: React has a built-in feature of being aware of the form and renders seamlessly in mobile and different web forms.

- **Rich Ecosystem**: There is a large community that supports and enhances React, providing many tools and methods to learn and implement React for complex web application development.

Understanding React would be critical for the success of learning the skills for developing a web application. There are plenty of sources on the web and Gen AI, which can help you learn the basic and advanced features of React.

CHAPTER 4   FRONT-END DEVELOPMENT

State Management with Redux

Another commonly used JavaScript library with React is Redux, which helps in data state management within your application. The simple way to understand the difference between the two is that React helps with user interfaces and Redux manages the data state of the application. Together, they offer a powerful way to manage large and complex applications where a huge load of data is being exchanged between multiple components of a React application. Some of the key benefits of Redux are listed below:

- The state of your application is stored in a single centralized immutable object globally accessible to all the DOM components of your React Application.
- Redux has a predefined set of functions called reducers, which are solely responsible for dispatching actions.
- As the state has a unidirectional flow, it makes data tracking and debugging easier.

The following are some of the key elements Redux uses:

- **Store** the entire application state as a JavaScript Object tree.
- All state changes are communicated through **Actions,** which are plain JavaScript Objects.
- **Reducers** are functions that take a current state and an action and transfer into a new object, without directly mutating the object – saving memory and hence higher performance.
- **Dispatch** function sends an action to the store to update the state of the object using reducers.
- **Selectors** help to extract specific data from the state, promoting a decouple component structure.
- There is also a **middleware** component that intercepts messages before they reach a reducer. This helps in creating custom logic and asynchronous operation management.

CHAPTER 4 FRONT-END DEVELOPMENT

State management is an important element of complex web application development. It is imperative that the state is managed well for smooth data flow and faster web page rendering for achieving a greater user experience.

Single-Page Application (SPA) Design

No learning about front-end development is complete without understanding the Single-Page Application (SPA) concept. As the name indicates, SPAs are a web application that loads a single HTML page and dynamically updates content based on user interaction. The best example of SPA is Gmail. As you navigate between different features of Gmail, such as a new email, inbox, and label folders, you must have noticed that the page doesn't refresh, but only the data updates.

SPA uses JavaScript to fetch the necessary data and update only the portion of the page that requires updating. The SPA design works in the following paradigm:

- For the first time, the browser downloads the HTML page, CSS, and JavaScript files.

- Next, based on the user interaction, using JavaScript, relevant content gets dynamically fetched. This is done using AJAX (Asynchronous JavaScript and XML), which communicates to the back-end server asynchronously.

- Data is exchanged between the application and the server in a particular format (JSON).

- Once the browser receives the data, a specific part of the DOM tree is updated with the new component/data content, and only the required part of the page is updated.

This helps to achieve an app-like experience right on the web browser. The following are some of the key benefits of SPA:

- **Intuitive User Experience**: A single-page HTML makes the interface simple and easy to understand. Designers can focus on user-friendly, intuitive design without worrying about refreshing the entire page from a performance standpoint.

41

- **Faster Loading Times**: As only the required part of the page is refreshed, the page loading is much faster. Besides, the server requests are asynchronous, allowing users to interact with multiple components on the page simultaneously.

- **Reduce Server Load**: Only the required data request is sent to the server (read as a subset), reducing the load on back-end operations dramatically. Also, as the requests are asynchronous, multiple threads can run at the same time for data fetching, providing built-in scaling capabilities.

- **Decoupling Front End and Back End**: SPA clearly demarks the HTML and CSS from the JavaScript – allowing greater maintainability of the code.

- **Cross-Platform Compatibility**: Natively, SPA helps to render content on multifactor forms, mobile platforms, and multiple browser versions and makes. You can code once and make it available across a multitude of content delivery platforms.

- **Offline Functionality**: SPA also supports caching options, which can make your web page available for offline viewing. Many input operations can be done offline, which syncs back to the server once you come back online.

Summary

In this chapter, we learned all the key elements – HTML, CSS, and JavaScript fundamentals – that are essential to learn for front-end development. We also learned about frameworks such as React.js and Redux, concepts such as SPA that are essential for complex web development. These are foundational skills, and mastering them is essential to becoming an expert in full-stack development.

CHAPTER 5

Database Management

Introduction

Modern-day web applications demand dynamic delivery, data rendition, and display of content. In a dynamic web application, content can come in many forms – it could be curated for user consumption (e.g., information about a place), transactional (e.g., buying history of a user), or user-generated (e.g., user comments or feedback). Modern-day web applications contain a multitude of content, which varies from simple text content to multimedia content such as video, audio, and images. Where the data will persist and how it will be accessed are critical design considerations one needs to take while defining a complex web application. An ideal design at a minimum should consider the following set of design principles:

- Data security and protocols used to securely transact and transfer data
- User experience to ensure maximum user retention
- Data transfer speed and methodologies used to adequately render data swiftly
- Data state management to minimize the load on the data server
- Data recovery, in case of failure

In our book, as we design the Half Time Whistle web application, we will undergo learning and implementing all these principles. MongoDB will store the details of places such as place name, date of visit, author's experience, related images (only names as images will be stored in CDN), and details on related places. These places will be retrieved by our application to render it for user consumption. We have chosen MongoDB as our primary back-end database technology. MongoDB is cloud native and

Chapter 5 Database Management

provides a reliable, scalable, and robust database that suits our web application needs. In this chapter, you will get introduced to the fundamentals of MongoDB and visit some of the best practices one should follow while considering a database for a web application.

MongoDB also offers a powerful solution for leveraging generative AI ecosystems for developing new-age AI-centric applications. MongoDB native vector storage and vector search provide seamless integration with large language models (LLMs) and retrieval-augmented generation (RAG) pipelines for creating an enterprise-grade solution. By combining flexible document storage, real-time analytics, and robust scalability, MongoDB can be leveraged to build AI-powered applications.

MongoDB Fundamentals

MongoDB is a cloud native NoSQL and document-oriented database that stores data in a flexible, JSON-like format called BSON. Data is organized into collections rather than traditional tables, which provides greater flexibility for handling unstructured or semi-structured data. We chose MongoDB as the data store for the following key reasons:

- MongoDB is not constrained to a set structure like traditional database modes. Its document-oriented structure allows to create a document within a document and with any number of fields and structures. This **flexible schema design** allows us to design our web page content template to evolve and vary based on the needs.

- Because of this flexible design, MongoDB supports **rapid application development,** where we can design our schema as we enhance our design. Its JSON-based object model is easy to consume for data rendition.

- As your application scales, MongoDB could **horizontally scale** through sharding concepts by distributing data across multiple data servers. The SaaS platform allows you to configure this by clicking a few buttons.

- As data are stored together in a collection, the **queries are faster** (minimum joins are required). It is also well supported by a robust **indexing** method that MongoDB offers.

- **MongoDB Query Language (MQL)** is intuitive, and JSON-based is easy to learn and execute.

- MongoDB is a **cloud native solution** that works on all major cloud providers including Azure, AWS, and Google Cloud, making it ubiquitously available with a large **active community**.

From a feature standpoint, MongoDB supports the following key concepts:

- A **document model** that can contain nested structures, arrays, objects, and fields of varying type. Data is stored as a JSON object with a field/value pair combination.

- When documents are grouped together, a **collection** is formed. You can compare collection to a table in relational database parlance.

- One MongoDB instance can have multiple **databases**, and each database can have its own set of collections.

- While storing data, MongoDB stores data as **Binary JSON (BSON)**. This helps in storing data optimally for secure and faster retrieval.

- Every MongoDB object has a system-generated **unique identifier(_id)**; it is a 12-byte primary key for each document object.

- MongoDB natively offers **replication (replica sets)** that provides high data availability and redundancy.

- MongoDB has a robust security mechanism. It uses SCRAM (Salted Challenge Response Authentication Mechanism)-based **authentication**, **role-based access** to data, **TLS/SSL**-based encryption, and details for security **audit** purposes.

These concepts collectively make MongoDB one of the top choices as a data store for complex web applications.

As a result of the technologies in our world rapidly expanding, a web application's average life span is just 2–3 years. That is why it's so important to adapt to the relevant technologies for your web application.

CHAPTER 5   DATABASE MANAGEMENT

Data Modeling

An adequate MongoDB data modeling is pertinent for the web application to demonstrate high response time while keeping proper design principles in mind to ensure elevated maintainability. Also, as your web application scales, you need to ensure your data store is capable of scaling both vertically as well as horizontally. Let us visit some key data modeling principles.

The most important design principle you need to consider is how your application will query data. Understanding your application needs is important as it has a direct impact on your application performance and stability.

Design Principle 1: Do you want to embed a document into a document, or do you want to use referencing?

- Embedding is putting all content within a document in a hierarchical structure. This is like denormalization in the relational database concept. If your document size is small and is frequently used together, embedding is the way to go, as it will access data at high speed. However, if your document size is large (16 MB is the limit) and if you update your content too often, embedding is not the right option. While embedding has advantages, there are trade-offs that one needs to be aware of. A few of the critical ones are mentioned below:

- Update to an embedded document is atomic. Either everything is changed or nothing.

- As embedded objects have everything together for a document, often embedding increases database size, increases inconsistencies, and increases the chance of duplicity.

- Querying embedded documents is easy and simple as it is all stored together

- However, indexing is a tricky affair, as the documents usually have deeply nested fields, which need extremely careful planning. If a large number of indexes are created, it could drastically slow down query performance.

CHAPTER 5 DATABASE MANAGEMENT

- Bulk update across multiple documents could be complex, slow, and redundant.

- Referencing usually makes the query slow as it has form joins between documents but it is best suited when the document size is large or updates happen too frequently.

Design Principle 2: Which pattern to use for data modeling

- **Flat Model**: If your dataset is small. In this model, all fields are in a single document.

- **Embedded Model**: Related data are all stored as embedded documents. This model is best when the relationships are few.

- **Referenced Model**: Related data are stored in separate documents. Best suited for large datasets and when you have many one-to-many relationships.

- **Hybrid Model**: A combination of embedded and referenced models. In our example, we have used the hybrid model.

Here is an example of a collection from our application. The collection name is **places,** and the document object stores data as a key/value pair. Note the unique ID generated by the system:

```json
JSON
{
  "_id": {
    "$oid": "6701fc0643a2d6577054b9b8"
  },
  "title": "Shenandoah National Park",
```

"description": "About 300 miles from NJ, Shenandoah National Park is 200,000 acres of sheer nature's beauty with cascading waterfalls, thickets that beckon tranquility, beds of wildflowers, spectacular vistas, and is home to many animal species such as deer, black bears, and many species of birds. The Shenandoah National Park is located between two states: the western part is in Virginia, and the eastern part is situated in the panhandle of West Virginia, and the entire park is located between the Blue Ridge and the Allegheny Mountain range."

CHAPTER 5   DATABASE MANAGEMENT

```
    "image": "shenandoah.jpg",
    "region": "northeast"
}
```

Query Optimization

When datasets in MongoDB get large, it is imperative to implement strategies to optimize the query performance so that data retrieval operations are fast and reliable. MongoDB inherently provides many different query optimization techniques, some of which are mentioned below:

- MongoDB offers **creation of indexes** – create an index on a field frequently used to find documents. For example, the example above **region** and **title** is often used by our application to locate places content and will be a good candidate to index. Also, create an index on which you usually sort the content.

- Determine what type of index you want to create.

  - **Single Field Indexes**: When queries are for individual fields.

  - **Compound Indexes**: For queries that involve multiple fields.

  - You can also index elements within an array. For this, you need to use **Multi-Key Indexes**.

  - **Text Index**: For full-text search.

  - **Geospatial Indexes**: For geographical data.

- Always index the query or the sort fields. **Avoid over-indexing**, as it slows write operations.

- You can also monitor **index usage** to gain insight into used and unused indexes.

- Focus on optimizing query structures.

  - Use **projection** to limit the fields returned by a query to reduce data transfer.

- Use **pagination** to retrieve data in small batches. You can use `limit()` to define how many records to return and `skip()` to skip certain records.

- Design queries to **utilize indexes** and **avoid complete collection scans**, as collection scans are costly resources.

- Use **regular expression (Regex) sparingly**, as it is resource-intensive.

- Implement pipeline optimization techniques such as

  - Place `$match` early in the pipeline to filter documents out as soon as possible.

  - Use `$project` to limit fields in the query.

  - Avoid unnecessary `$group` as it is resource-intensive. You can always get the record to the front end and use JavaScript to do content manipulation.

  - Always filter data first before using `$lookup` for joining collections.

- Finally, there are other optimization techniques that you can implement for your applications. Some of them are listed below:

  - You can use **caching** to store frequently accessed data. This reduces the number of queries to the back-end database.

  - When you have large datasets, you can distribute your data collection across servers by using **sharding**. Your queries can then be processed in parallel, increasing performance.

  - Choosing the **right data types** is equally important for faster performance.

Another important aspect of query optimization is query performance analysis. MongoDB offers native tools such as the explain() method, which provides detailed insights on how the query is executed, details on the index used, and details on documents scanned.

CHAPTER 5   DATABASE MANAGEMENT

Besides the explan() method, other best practices include regular profiling, leveraging caching for frequently accessed data, and refactoring data models to align with actual query patterns.

These are some of the best practices you can implement to ensure you create the right data model, optimize queries, and use the right index principles.

Database Security

While web applications have opened a new frontier to connect to your target audience on a global platform, it has also resulted in having many malicious bots and users crawling the web world, stealing information. Particularly, if you deal with sensitive data such as user personal information, health records, or credit card and financial details, protecting your data becomes a core part of your design strategy. MongoDB offers many built-in mechanisms to protect your data, and as a good full-stack developer, we need to not only orient the features but also implement them wisely. Listed below are some of the comprehensive ways you can keep your MongoDB data secure:

Authentication: The first step in getting your environment secure is to get your user identity secure. Authentication allows users to connect to the MongoDB database. The following are some of the available authentication mechanisms:

- **SCRAM (Salted Challenge Response Authentication Mechanism)**: This is the default MongoDB challenge response authentication method. User passwords are securely transmitted and stored by MongoDB.

- **Using TSL/SSL Certificates**: This is suitable for a highly secure access environment using PKI (Public Key Infrastructure).

- You can also integrate your MongoDB authentication with existing **LDAP** directories.

- **Kerberos** authentication for Single Sign-On is also available for a highly secure corporate environment.

- Finally, you can use external authentication with **OAuth** providers such as GitHub, Google, and others.

Authorization: After authentication, you need authorization to determine who has what kind of access. MongoDB offers role-based access to manage privileges.

- Roles contain specific privileges to do certain work. For example, you don't want to give admin access to everyone.

- Privileges are a set of actions you assign to a role (Read, Write, Update, and Delete).

- The best practice is always to start with the least privilege for a role that is necessary to do a particular function. There are built-in roles that MongoDB offers that could be leveraged for certain operational, admin, and maintenance roles.

Data Encryption: As data remain in MongoDB (at rest) or move between the database server and application (in motion), we need to adopt the right principles to ensure data is always safeguarded.

- Use TLS/SSL while the data is in transit to prevent unauthorized access and possible data tampering.

- MongoDB offers WiredTiger storage engine encryption to protect data at rest.

- MongoDB also provides Key Management Service (KMS) for managing encryption keys.

- You can also protect data at the client side before it is sent over to MongoDB using Client-Side Field Level Encryption (CSFLE).

All these data encryption features could be leveraged to ensure data is well protected, both in motion and at rest, from malicious activities. The MongoDB community has fewer security features available as compared to the enterprise edition, which offers a robust authentication mechanism and enhanced encryption.

It's important to have strong security behind your databases, as there has been a 78% increase in data breach incidents from the years 2022 to 2023.

CHAPTER 5   DATABASE MANAGEMENT

Data Persistence Strategies

You may have the unfortunate circumstance where your data is corrupted or lost because of human error, system glitches, or malicious intent. In such scenarios, your ability to recover lost data would become crucial. MongoDB offers a wide range of data persistence and backup capabilities. Some of these strategies are listed below:

- In disaster scenarios, MongoDB leverages the oplog (Operations log) to enable point-in-time recovery (PITR). Oplog keeps a complete track of CRUD operations in the exact order on the primary node. In this approach, the last full snapshot of the database is used, followed by sequentially restoring the incremental updates using the oplog.

- MongoDB Atlas provides a robust solution for data protection, disaster recovery, and backup. Atlas Backup leverages the underlying cloud provider to create consistent, cluster-wide snapshots at scheduled intervals depending on user-defined retention policies. The system supports both snapshot-based backups, which capture the state of the database at a specific point in time, and point-in-time recovery (PITR), allowing restoration to any moment within a configured backup window.

- Although MongoDB is cloud-based and provides native backup capabilities, it is a great idea to regularly back up your data. You can use `mongodump` for smaller datasets, and for larger databases, use **filesystem snapshots**. These backups could be scheduled or used on an ad hoc basis. You can create cron jobs or write Python scripts to be scheduled and run by an orchestrator tool such as Ansible.

- It is a good practice to validate your backup regularly by restoring from backup to see if your backup is working fine. You can create a different database to test your backup validation.

- If your web application generates massive amounts of data and if some of the data is transactional and you need it only for a transient period, consider implementing retention policies. Retention periods are often mandated by regulatory requirements (depending on the type of data you are storing), and it is a good practice to ensure such policies are adhered to before you permanently purge any data.

- Consider compressing data and encrypting them at rest to save space and to protect sensitive content.

- You can leverage MongoDB replica sets to maintain multiple copies of data. This will enable high availability for your web application.

- If you are leveraging MongoDB sharding, the backups must be coordinated among the sharded clusters to maintain consistency.

Summary

Understanding and appreciating database management is important for building a scalable and robust web application. MongoDB offers a multitude of built-in functionalities to deploy a data model that can be queried for faster retrieval of data. Concepts such as indexing, database security, and data persistence techniques help you to create a data bedrock that is secure and reliable. Apply these principles and practices as you create your web application. Some of these elements you will see in practice in the subsequent chapters.

CHAPTER 6

Gen AI in Web Development

Introduction

Ever since Gen AI was first introduced in 2021, when OpenAI provided the first version of ChatGPT, the technology world has never remained the same. Gen AI is a strong leap from traditional AI, for AI in general has been analysis, classification, and prediction based on some existing data. On the contrary, Gen AI is first trained on large data sets, then it understands the complex relationship between content, and finally produces completely new content based on that learning, which is different from the training data. These contents can be text, video, audio, images, and software code.

Did you know? It only took five days for ChatGPT to gain one million users! Compared to Instagram, which took one month to gain one million users, or even Facebook, which took ten months, we can see how much our world is drastically changing with the advancements of AI tools. As of 2025, around 700 million people use ChatGPT weekly, which doesn't even take into account other LLMs!

In this chapter, we will understand the fundamentals of Gen AI and how we can leverage them for code development in the context of a web application. There are a multitude of Gen AI-enabled environments available, such as Cursor and Replit, which can be leveraged for code generation. You can also use LLM models like ChatGPT, Perplexity, and Gemini to generate code. While Cursor and Claude are deeply trained in software programming, the other Gen AIs are equally capable of generating code.

Gen AI used deep learning like Generative Adversarial Networks (GANs), Variational Autoencoders (VAEs), and transformer-based models to generate new and novel content. This chapter will further focus on concepts such as prompt engineering, AI-assisted coding, and debugging to provide a good grounding in the fundamentals of leveraging AI to intelligently generate code and debug it.

While Gen AI has extremely evolved to help navigate the complex programming landscape, it also comes with several limitations. Before using Gen AI for coding, one should be completely aware of the same so that the right guardrails can be put in place. Some of the key ones are mentioned below:

- AI-generated code may appear syntactically correct but can have subtle bugs, performance concerns, and security vulnerabilities.

- AI-generated code often ignores complex and ambiguous conditions and patterns, making the code erroneous for edge cases.

- AI-generated code is sometimes limited by the training data and may not always adhere to architectural best practices.

- AI code can also introduce bias based on the data on which the model is trained.

- AI code may sometimes have compliance issues when it uses code with intellectual property (IP) concerns.

It is always advised for humans to read, understand, and thoroughly examine/review all AI-generated code before pushing to production.

Prompt Engineering Techniques

To adequately leverage Gen AI to create code, you need to appreciate, understand, and implement prompt engineering techniques. The adage "Garbage in, Garbage Out" is quite apt in this context, for a prompt that is not adequately designed and thought through may result in output that either may not provide the correct code (or any other content) or erroneous code that may derail your project.

Prompt engineering is a combination of both art and science – the prompts you offer to the Gen AI model need to be designed and fine-tuned to ensure the LLMs (large language models) accurately comprehend them to generate a well-crafted response. The goal of prompt engineering is to reduce ambiguity, minimize the chance of hallucinations (hallucinations are when the LLMs provide inadequate and inconsistent output), and ensure the LLMs provide you with concise, to-the-point answers to your queries. However, please note that while the LLM would give us code, developers should validate the authenticity, logic, security, and usability of the code. Use this as a tool to accelerate coding, not a replacement for human supervision and guidance. Let us understand a few prompt engineering techniques in the section below.

Zero-Shot Prompting

This is the most basic form of prompting, where you ask the model to answer a question without providing any context. The model answers the question based on the pre-trained knowledge.

This model is best fit when your query is for general knowledge and the LLM's knowledge is sufficient to answer it.

Example Prompt

Create a simple React "Hello World Example" where a function prints Hello World on the web Page

```
import React from 'react';
function HelloWorld() {
      return (
             <h1>Hello, World!</h1>
      );
}
export default HelloWorld;
```

Few-Shot Prompting

In few-shot prompting, the prompt will have a few examples of input/output pairs to guide the LLMs to provide a desired output.

Example Prompt: Below is the prompt you would send to the language model. It includes a few labeled examples and then the user's input.

Classify the sentiment of the following statements as "positive", "negative", or "neutral".

CHAPTER 6   GEN AI IN WEB DEVELOPMENT

Statement: "I love using this app, it's fantastic!"

Sentiment: positive

Statement: "This app is really hard to use."

Sentiment: negative

Statement: "The app is okay, nothing special."

Sentiment: neutral

Statement: "{user_input}"

Sentiment:

LLM Output

The output below is a simple React component that demonstrates how this prompt uses the OpenAI API:

```
import React, { useState } from "react";

const FEW_SHOT_PROMPT = `
Classify the sentiment of the following statements as "positive", "negative", or "neutral".

Statement: "I love using this app, it's fantastic!"
Sentiment: positive

Statement: "This app is really hard to use."
Sentiment: negative

Statement: "The app is okay, nothing special."
Sentiment: neutral

Statement: "{input}"
Sentiment:
`;

function FewShotSentiment() {
  const [statement, setStatement] = useState("");
  const [sentiment, setSentiment] = useState("");
  const [loading, setLoading] = useState(false);
```

```
const handleSubmit = async (e) => {
  e.preventDefault();
  setLoading(true);
  setSentiment("");

  const prompt = FEW_SHOT_PROMPT.replace("{input}", statement);

  const response = await fetch("https://api.openai.com/v1/completions", {
    method: "POST",
    headers: {
      "Content-Type": "application/json",
      Authorization: `Bearer ${process.env.REACT_APP_OPENAI_API_KEY}`,
    },
    body: JSON.stringify({
      model: "text-davinci-003",
      prompt,
      max_tokens: 10,
      temperature: 0,
    }),
  });

  const data = await response.json();
  setSentiment(data.choices[0].text.trim());
  setLoading(false);
};

return (
  <div>
    <h2>Sentiment Classifier (Few-Shot Prompting)</h2>
    <form onSubmit={handleSubmit}>
      <input
        value={statement}
        onChange={(e) => setStatement(e.target.value)}
        placeholder="Enter a statement"
      />
      <button type="submit" disabled={loading}>
        Classify
```

```
        </button>
      </form>
      {loading && <p>Loading...</p>}
      {sentiment && (
        <div>
          <strong>Sentiment:</strong> {sentiment}
        </div>
      )}
    </div>
  );
}

export default FewShotSentiment;
```

Chain-of-Thought Prompting

In chain-of-thought prompting, you ask the LLM model to reason based on the step-by-step instructions provided as a prompt.

Example Prompt

I need a React component that fetches a list of users from an API and displays them. Think step by step as provided below:

1. How should I manage loading and error states?

2. What React Hook should I use for data fetching?

3. How do I display the list of users?

4. How do I handle potential errors during fetching?

LLM Output

```
Thought:
1. For loading and error states, I'll use `useState` hooks to manage
   `isLoading` and `error` boolean/string states. This allows me to
   conditionally render UI based on these states.
2. For data fetching, `useEffect` is the appropriate hook. It allows
   performing side effects (like data fetching) after render, and I'll
   ensure it runs only once on mount with an empty dependency array.
```

3. To display the list, I'll use `map` over the `users` array (also managed with `useState`) to render individual `UserItem` components or simply list items.
4. Error handling will involve a `try-catch` block within the `fetch` operation. If an error occurs, I'll set the `error` state and display an error message to the user.

Action: Generate the `UserList` component.

```jsx
import React, { useState, useEffect } from 'react';

function UserList() {
  const [users, setUsers] = useState([]);
  const [isLoading, setIsLoading] = useState(true);
  const [error, setError] = useState(null);

  useEffect(() => {
    const fetchUsers = async () => {
      try {
        const response = await fetch('[https://jsonplaceholder.typicode.com/users](https://jsonplaceholder.typicode.com/users)');
        // Example API
        if (!response.ok) {
          throw new Error(`HTTP error! status: ${response.status}`);
        }
        const data = await response.json();
        setUsers(data);
      } catch (err) {
        setError(err.message);
      } finally {
        setIsLoading(false);
      }
    };

    fetchUsers();
  }, []); // Empty dependency array means this effect runs once on mount
```

```
  if (isLoading) {
    return <div>Loading users...</div>;
  }

  if (error) {
    return <div>Error: {error}</div>;
  }

  return (
    <div>
      <h1>User List</h1>
      <ul>
        {users.map(user => (
          <li key={user.id}>
            <strong>{user.name}</strong> ({user.email})
          </li>
        ))}
      </ul>
    </div>
  );
}

export default UserList;
```

Asking the LLM to explain something to you step by step has been shown to boost reasoning accuracy!

Role-Play/Persona Prompting

You can make your LLM AI model assume a particular persona and provide responses. Using this approach sharpens the response to a particular style, tone, and authority, making your responses more tailored to your context.

CHAPTER 6 GEN AI IN WEB DEVELOPMENT

Following a role-play or persona prompt sometimes works better than just giving out instructions! The AI is able to adapt to the tone you want, delve into specific details, and even give you better examples.

Prompt Example

You are a senior React architect. Your key focus is creating optimized code with a deep focus on nonfunctional requirements (NFR) such as performance and security. You produce clean and readable code with comments for easier understanding. You also do proper error handling for all scenarios.

Now, create a reusable function that takes a Boolean input to make a button enabled or disabled. Also, the button color should change based on the color provided by user. If no color is offered default is Blue for Enabled button and Gray for Disabled button.

Prompt Output

The following is the output provided by the LLM model:

```
import React from 'react';
import PropTypes from 'prop-types';

/**
 * ReusableButton Component
 *
 * Props:
 * - isEnabled (Boolean): Determines if the button is enabled or disabled.
 * - color (String, optional): The color for the enabled button. Defaults to blue.
 * - onClick (Function, optional): Callback for button click. Only fires if enabled.
 * - children (Node): Button label/content.
 */
const ReusableButton = ({
  isEnabled,
  color,
  onClick,
  children,
  ...rest
```

```jsx
}) => {
  // Default colors
  const enabledColor = color || '#2563eb'; // Tailwind Blue-600
  const disabledColor = '#9ca3af'; // Tailwind Gray-400

  // Inline style for button
  const buttonStyle = {
    backgroundColor: isEnabled ? enabledColor : disabledColor,
    color: '#fff',
    border: 'none',
    borderRadius: 4,
    padding: '0.5em 1.5em',
    cursor: isEnabled ? 'pointer' : 'not-allowed',
    transition: 'background-color 0.2s',
    outline: 'none'
  };

  // Secure click handler: only fires if enabled
  const handleClick = (e) => {
    try {
      if (isEnabled && typeof onClick === 'function') {
        onClick(e);
      }
    } catch (error) {
      // Optional: Log error or handle gracefully
      console.error('Button click error:', error);
    }
  };

  return (
    <button
      type="button"
      style={buttonStyle}
      disabled={!isEnabled}
      aria-disabled={!isEnabled}
      onClick={handleClick}
      {...rest}
```

```
    >
      {children}
    </button>
  );
};
// PropTypes for robust type checking
ReusableButton.propTypes = {
  isEnabled: PropTypes.bool.isRequired,
  color: PropTypes.string,
  onClick: PropTypes.func,
  children: PropTypes.node.isRequired,
};
export default ReusableButton;
```

You can call the above function using the below code.

```
<ReusableButton
  isEnabled={true}
  color="#16a34a" // Optional: custom green
  onClick={() => alert('Button clicked!')}
>
  Click Me
</ReusableButton>
```

Instruction-Based Prompting

As the name indicates, in this kind of prompting, the instructions need to be clear and precise. The prompt appears more like a command to the AI. The LLM model then understands the instructions and executes it without needing much task-specific training data.

Prompt Example

Generate a React component for a controlled input field.
It should:

CHAPTER 6   GEN AI IN WEB DEVELOPMENT

- Give it a name of your choice
- input and validate for email address.
- use font dark gray and font size 16 as soon as user loses focus from the text box.

Prompt Output

```
import React, { useState } from 'react';

/**
 * EmailInputField Component
 * Controlled input for email with validation and dynamic styling.
 */
const EmailInputField = () => {
  // State for input value and validation error
  const [email, setEmail] = useState('');
  const [error, setError] = useState('');
  const [isBlurred, setIsBlurred] = useState(false);

  // Email validation regex (simple version)
  const emailRegex = /^[^\s@]+@[^\s@]+\.[^\s@]+$/;

  // Handle input change
  const handleChange = (e) => {
    setEmail(e.target.value);
    setError(''); // Reset error on change
  };

  // Handle blur event for validation and styling
  const handleBlur = () => {
    setIsBlurred(true);

    // Validate email format
    if (email.length === 0) {
      setError('Email is required.');
    } else if (!emailRegex.test(email)) {
      setError('Please enter a valid email address.');
    } else {
      setError('');
```

```
    }
};

// Dynamic style for input after blur
const inputStyle = isBlurred
  ? { color: '#1a1a1a', fontSize: 16 } // Dark gray and 16px
  : {};

return (
  <div style={{ marginBottom: '1em' }}>
    <label htmlFor="email-input" style={{ display: 'block',
    marginBottom: 4 }}>
      Email Address
    </label>
    <input
      id="email-input"
      type="email"
      value={email}
      onChange={handleChange}
      onBlur={handleBlur}
      style={{
        ...inputStyle,
        padding: '8px 12px',
        border: error ? '1px solid #e11d48' : '1px solid #d1d5db',
        borderRadius: 4,
        outline: 'none',
        width: '100%',
        boxSizing: 'border-box',
        transition: 'border-color 0.2s',
      }}
      aria-invalid={!!error}
      aria-describedby="email-error"
      autoComplete="email"
      placeholder="Enter your email"
    />
    {error && (
```

```
        <div
          id="email-error"
          style={{ color: '#e11d48', fontSize: 14, marginTop: 4 }}
          role="alert"
        >
          {error}
        </div>
      )}
    </div>
  );
};

export default EmailInputField;
```

Output Formatting/Constraint Prompting

In this kind of prompting, you instruct the AI to generate output based on your required template, format, structure, and constraints. This kind of prompting is particularly useful when you want output in a particular format that you can immediately use without any modification.

Prompt Example

Create a React component named `UserInfo`.

It must return JSX wrapped in a single div. Please use the class name for the div as user-block.

The Div should display the following elements

- A title of font Arial-Bold size 14 color dark blue and style H2

- A paragraph of font Arial size 12 color black

Prompt Output

```
import React from 'react';

const UserInfo = () => {
  return (
    <div className="user-block">
      <h2
```

```
    style={{
      fontFamily: 'Arial, Arial-Bold, sans-serif',
      fontWeight: 'bold',
      fontSize: 14,
      color: '#003366', // Dark blue
      margin: 0,
    }}
  >
    User Information
  </h2>
  <p
    style={{
      fontFamily: 'Arial, sans-serif',
      fontSize: 12,
      color: '#000000',
      marginTop: 8,
    }}
  >
    This section contains user details and relevant information.
  </p>
  </div>
 );
};

export default UserInfo;
```

Generated Knowledge Prompting

Generated knowledge prompting is a two-step process. First, you ask the AI to generate related background information on the topic, and then you ask the AI to generate the response to your question. This approach helps the LLM to understand the context of the question better and provide a better and more relevant response.

Prompt Example

First, explain what is JSON.stringify in context to React.js, and then generate a JSON. stringify to publish some sample metadata.

Prompt Output

What is JSON.stringify in React.js?

In the context of React.js, JSON.stringify is a JavaScript method used to convert a JavaScript object, array, or value into a JSON string representation. This is particularly useful in React for:

Sending data to APIs: Many web APIs expect data in JSON string format.

Storing state or props: For example, saving data to localStorage or debugging by logging state as a string.

Displaying structured data: Sometimes you want to render an object as a readable string in the UI.

The syntax is:

js

JSON.stringify(value, replacer, space)

value: The object or value to convert.

replacer (optional): Function or array to filter properties.

space (optional): Adds indentation for readability.

Example: Publishing Sample Metadata with JSON.stringify

Suppose you have some sample metadata about a user or a document. Here's how you would use JSON.stringify to convert it to a JSON string for publishing or transmission:

```js
const metadata = {
  id: "12345",
  title: "Sample Document",
  author: "Jane Doe",
  createdAt: new Date().toISOString(),
  tags: ["react", "json", "metadata"]
};

const jsonString = JSON.stringify(metadata, null, 2); // Pretty print with 2 spaces

console.log(jsonString);
```

Self-Consistency Prompting

In this type of prompting, you ask the AI to give you multiple answers to the prompt and then ask the AI to critically evaluate the options and ask it to choose one for you. This type of prompting may require multiple prompts or may need an agentic setup.

Prompt Example

Generate three different ways to represent an image carousel using React.js. Please consider the following:

- The images should be quickly rendered
- Ease of moving between images
- Form factor consideration

After generating the code critically evaluate the options for simplicity, performance, and other best practices. Also, provide a detail explanation on your choice at the end.

Prompt Output

Here are three different ways to implement an image carousel in React.js, each designed for fast image rendering, easy navigation, and responsive layouts. After the code, you'll find a critical evaluation and a clear recommendation.

1. **Basic Custom Carousel with React Hooks**

    This version uses React's built-in state and effect hooks for a lightweight, dependency-free carousel.

    ```jsx
    import React, { useState, useEffect } from 'react';

    const images = [
      { id: 1, url: 'https://images.pexels.com/photos/29089597/pexels-photo-29089597.jpeg' },
      { id: 2, url: 'https://images.pexels.com/photos/691668/pexels-photo-691668.jpeg' },
      { id: 3, url: 'https://images.pexels.com/photos/2049422/pexels-photo-2049422.jpeg' },
    ];

    const BasicCarousel = () => {
      const [current, setCurrent] = useState(0);
    ```

```jsx
  useEffect(() => {
    const timer = setTimeout(() => setCurrent((current + 1) %
    images.length), 5000);
    return () => clearTimeout(timer);
  }, [current]);

  const prev = () => setCurrent(current === 0 ? images.length - 1
: current - 1);
  const next = () => setCurrent((current + 1) % images.length);

  return (
    <div style={{ maxWidth: 600, margin: 'auto', position:
    'relative' }}>
      <img
        src={images[current].url}
        alt=""
        style={{ width: '100%', height: 350, objectFit: 'cover',
        borderRadius: 10 }}
        loading="lazy"
      />
      <button onClick={prev} style={{ position: 'absolute', top:
      '50%', left: 10 }}>{"<"}</button>
      <button onClick={next} style={{ position: 'absolute', top:
      '50%', right: 10 }}>{">"}</button>
    </div>
  );
};

export default BasicCarousel;
```

2. **Carousel Using a Popular Library**

    This approach uses a ready-made carousel component for advanced features and responsive design.

    ```jsx
    import React from 'react';
    import Slider from 'react-slick';
    import 'slick-carousel/slick/slick.css';
    ```

```
import 'slick-carousel/slick/slick-theme.css';

const images = [
  { id: 1, url: 'https://images.pexels.com/photos/29089597/pexels-
  photo-29089597.jpeg' },
  { id: 2, url: 'https://images.pexels.com/photos/691668/pexels-
  photo-691668.jpeg' },
  { id: 3, url: 'https://images.pexels.com/photos/2049422/pexels-
  photo-2049422.jpeg' },
];

const SlickCarousel = () => {
  const settings = {
    dots: true,
    infinite: true,
    speed: 500,
    slidesToShow: 1,
    slidesToScroll: 1,
    lazyLoad: 'ondemand',
    arrows: true,
    responsive: [
      { breakpoint: 600, settings: { arrows: false, dots: true } }
    ]
  };

  return (
    <div style={{ maxWidth: 600, margin: 'auto' }}>
      <Slider {...settings}>
        {images.map((img) => (
          <div key={{img.id}}>
            <img
              src={{img.url}}
              alt=""
              style={{ width: '100%', height: 350, objectFit:
              'cover', borderRadius: 10 }}
              loading="lazy"
            />
```

```jsx
        </div>
      ))}
    </Slider>
  </div>
  );
};

export default SlickCarousel;
```

3. **Horizontal Scroll Carousel (Touch-Friendly)**

   This version uses horizontal scrolling for a mobile-friendly, touch-first experience.

   ```jsx
   import React from 'react';

   const images = [
     { id: 1, url: 'https://images.pexels.com/photos/29089597/pexels-photo-29089597.jpeg' },
     { id: 2, url: 'https://images.pexels.com/photos/691668/pexels-photo-691668.jpeg' },
     { id: 3, url: 'https://images.pexels.com/photos/2049422/pexels-photo-2049422.jpeg' },
   ];

   const ScrollCarousel = () => (
     <div
       style={{
         display: 'flex',
         overflowX: 'auto',
         scrollSnapType: 'x mandatory',
         gap: 16,
         padding: 8,
         maxWidth: 600,
         margin: 'auto'
       }}
     >
       {images.map((img) => (
   ```

```
      <img
        key={img.id}
        src={img.url}
        alt=""
        style={{
          flex: '0 0 auto',
          width: 300,
          height: 200,
          objectFit: 'cover',
          borderRadius: 10,
          scrollSnapAlign: 'center'
        }}
        loading="lazy"
      />
    ))}
  </div>
);

export default ScrollCarousel;
```

Critical Evaluation

Approach	Simplicity	Performance	Responsiveness	Accessibility	Features	Best Use Case
Basic Custom	High	High	Good	Good	Basic navigation	Lightweight, custom styling needed
Library	Medium	Very High	Excellent	Excellent	Dots, swipes, arrows	Feature-rich, fast, responsive
Horizontal Scroll	Very High	High	Excellent	Basic	Touch, mobile-first	Mobile-first, minimal UI, fast loads

- The basic custom carousel is easy to understand and modify, making it ideal for simple needs or learning purposes. It's lightweight and can be styled as needed but lacks advanced features.

- The library-based carousel offers a full set of features, including navigation dots, swiping, and responsive design. It's optimized for performance and accessibility, making it suitable for production use.

- The horizontal scroll carousel is the simplest and most mobile-friendly. It's fast and easy to implement but doesn't include navigation buttons, which may be less ideal for desktop users.

Recommendation

For most production scenarios, the library-based carousel is the best choice. It provides a robust set of features, excellent performance, and strong support for accessibility and responsiveness. If your project is mobile-focused and you want the simplest, fastest solution, the horizontal scroll approach is ideal. For prototypes, learning, or when you want full control, the custom carousel is a solid option.

Tree-of-Thought Prompting

Tree-of-Thought prompting is the most evolved form of prompting. In this, we ask the LLM model to create multiple reasoning paths, evaluate them based on our criteria, and then instruct the LLM to select the right option for you.

This method allows the LLM model to create reasoning like a branching tree instead of a single linear path, and by doing so, it can evaluate multiple paths in parallel, brainstorm like a human, and finally come to a definitive conclusion.

LangChain is an implementation of Tree-of-Thought prompting through the use of classes such as the ToTChain. ToTChain uses the Tree-of-Thought and multiple solution paths to backtrack and compare alternatives to solve complex problems.

Prompt Example

We will use the same prompt from Self-Consistency Prompting to generate a Tree-of-Thought Prompt for Image Carousel in React.js. Below we will break down the task into clear steps and branches so that we can arrive at the best solution

Step 1: Identify Three Distinct Approaches

- **Branch 1:** Consider creating a custom carousel using only React's built-in hooks and features. Focus on fast rendering, simple navigation controls, and responsive design.

- **Branch 2:** Think about implementing a carousel using a well-known React carousel library. Aim for advanced navigation, built-in performance optimizations, and strong adaptability to different devices.

- **Branch 3:** Explore a solution that uses horizontal scrolling (using CSS overflow) to create a touch-friendly, mobile-first carousel. Prioritize simplicity, quick load times, and native scrolling.

Step 2: Implement Each Approach

- For each approach, outline the main logic and structure.
- Write concise and clear React code for each carousel, ensuring comments for readability.

Step 3: Critically Evaluate Each Solution

- Assess each approach for:
  - Simplicity and ease of understanding
  - Performance and speed of image rendering
  - Responsiveness and suitability for different screen sizes
  - Maintainability and alignment with best practices

Step 4: Make a Recommendation

- Analyze which approach offers the best balance of simplicity, performance, and modern development practices.
- Clearly explain your reasoning for choosing the most suitable method for a React image carousel.

Instruction: Work through each step and branch, generating three distinct carousel implementations in React, evaluating them, and providing a well-justified recommendation at the end.

Chapter 6 Gen AI in Web Development

Example Output
Step 1: Identify Three Distinct Approaches

- **Branch 1:** Custom Carousel using React hooks
- **Branch 2:** Carousel using a popular React library
- **Branch 3:** Carousel using horizontal scroll for mobile-first design

Step 2: Implement Each Approach
Branch 1: Custom Carousel with React Hooks

```jsx
import React, { useState, useEffect } from 'react';

const images = [
  { id: 1, url: 'https://images.pexels.com/photos/29089597/pexels-photo-29089597.jpeg' },
  { id: 2, url: 'https://images.pexels.com/photos/691668/pexels-photo-691668.jpeg' },
  { id: 3, url: 'https://images.pexels.com/photos/2049422/pexels-photo-2049422.jpeg' },
];

const CustomCarousel = () => {
  const [current, setCurrent] = useState(0);

  // Auto-advance every 5 seconds
  useEffect(() => {
    const timer = setTimeout(() => setCurrent((current + 1) % images.length), 5000);
    return () => clearTimeout(timer);
  }, [current]);

  const prev = () => setCurrent(current === 0 ? images.length - 1 : current - 1);
  const next = () => setCurrent((current + 1) % images.length);

  return (
    <div style={{ maxWidth: 600, margin: 'auto', position: 'relative' }}>
      <img
```

```jsx
      src={images[current].url}
      alt=""
      style={{ width: '100%', height: 350, objectFit: 'cover',
      borderRadius: 10 }}
      loading="lazy"
    />
    <button onClick={prev} style={{ position: 'absolute', top: '50%',
    left: 10 }}>{"<"}</button>
    <button onClick={next} style={{ position: 'absolute', top: '50%',
    right: 10 }}>{">"}</button>
  </div>
  );
};

export default CustomCarousel;
```

Branch 2: Carousel Using a Popular Library

```jsx
import React from 'react';
import Slider from 'react-slick';
import 'slick-carousel/slick/slick.css';
import 'slick-carousel/slick/slick-theme.css';

const images = [
  { id: 1, url: 'https://images.pexels.com/photos/29089597/pexels-photo-29089597.jpeg' },
  { id: 2, url: 'https://images.pexels.com/photos/691668/pexels-photo-691668.jpeg' },
  { id: 3, url: 'https://images.pexels.com/photos/2049422/pexels-photo-2049422.jpeg' },
];

const LibraryCarousel = () => {
  const settings = {
    dots: true,
    infinite: true,
    speed: 500,
```

```jsx
    slidesToShow: 1,
    slidesToScroll: 1,
    lazyLoad: 'ondemand',
    arrows: true,
    responsive: [
      { breakpoint: 600, settings: { arrows: false, dots: true } }
    ]
  };

  return (
    <div style={{ maxWidth: 600, margin: 'auto' }}>
      <Slider {...settings}>
        {images.map((img) => (
          <div key={img.id}>
            <img
              src={img.url}
              alt=""
              style={{ width: '100%', height: 350, objectFit: 'cover',
              borderRadius: 10 }}
              loading="lazy"
            />
          </div>
        ))}
      </Slider>
    </div>
  );
};

export default LibraryCarousel;
```

Branch 3: Horizontal Scroll Carousel (Mobile-First)

```jsx
import React from 'react';

const images = [
  { id: 1, url: 'https://images.pexels.com/photos/29089597/pexels-photo-29089597.jpeg' },
```

```
  { id: 2, url: 'https://images.pexels.com/photos/691668/pexels-
  photo-691668.jpeg' },
  { id: 3, url: 'https://images.pexels.com/photos/2049422/pexels-
  photo-2049422.jpeg' },
];

const ScrollCarousel = () => (
  <div
    style={{
      display: 'flex',
      overflowX: 'auto',
      scrollSnapType: 'x mandatory',
      gap: 16,
      padding: 8,
      maxWidth: 600,
      margin: 'auto'
    }}
  >
    {images.map((img) => (
      <img
        key={img.id}
        src={img.url}
        alt=""
        style={{
          flex: '0 0 auto',
          width: 300,
          height: 200,
          objectFit: 'cover',
          borderRadius: 10,
          scrollSnapAlign: 'center'
        }}
        loading="lazy"
      />
    ))}
  </div>
);
```

```
export default ScrollCarousel;
```

Step 3: Critical Evaluation

Approach	Simplicity	Performance	Responsiveness	Navigation	Best Use Case
Custom Carousel	High	High	Good	Buttons	Lightweight, custom styling
Library Carousel	Medium	Very High	Excellent	Dots, swipes, arrows	Feature-rich, production apps
Scroll Carousel	Very High	High	Excellent	Touch/scroll	Mobile-first, minimal UI

- **Custom Carousel:**
  - Simple to understand and modify.
  - Fast rendering with direct control.
  - Lacks advanced features like swipe or dots unless you add them.
- **Library Carousel:**
  - Offers advanced navigation (dots, swipes, arrows) and is highly responsive.
  - Handles lazy loading and edge cases out of the box.
  - Slightly more setup and dependency on third-party code.
- **Scroll Carousel:**
  - Easiest and fastest for mobile/touch devices.
  - Minimal code uses native scrolling.
  - No navigation buttons, so less ideal for desktop-heavy interfaces.

Step 4: Recommendation

For most modern applications, the **library-based carousel** is the best choice. It provides a robust set of features, excellent performance, and adapts well to different screen sizes and user interactions. It's especially suitable for production environments where accessibility, responsiveness, and a polished user experience are priorities.

If you want a lightweight, easily customizable solution for a simple use case, the **custom carousel** is a strong option. For mobile-first or content-heavy apps where simplicity and speed are key, the **horizontal scroll carousel** stands out.

Comparing All Prompts

Technique	Key Strengths	Typical Limitations/ Warnings
Zero-Shot Prompting	This is fast and simple and good for common queries.	Usually lacks accuracy as it is limited in prompt details.
Few-Shot Prompting	In this, you provide the model guidance on how to style/format the output.	Effort needs to be spent to design related examples.
Chain-of-Thought	In this, you make the model think logically by providing more inputs for a complex task, and hence, it can determine the reasoning process.	As the prompt becomes more verbose, it might introduce confusion.
Role-Play/ Persona	In this prompt, the tone is tailored. The prompt focuses on NFRs and domain constraints.	Risks over-narrow focus or overlooked requirements.
Instruction-Based	Directs LLM to a very specific outcome, thus minimizing ambiguity.	Output depends entirely on prompt clarity.
Output Formatting/ Constraint	Since the format is provided, the usability is immediate.	Rigid outputs and is not ideal for "open-ended" tasks.
Generated Knowledge	Contextualizes, improves depth and accuracy.	Multistep, could be verbose or off-topic.
Self-Consistency	Diverse options, critical evaluation, may avoid hallucinations.	Longer prompts may need an agentic setup.
Tree-of-Thought	Comprehensive, explores alternatives, strong deliberation	Increases response size and complexity.

CHAPTER 6   GEN AI IN WEB DEVELOPMENT

> Using reverse psychology on the LLM might also be something you would want to try out. Saying a prompt along the lines of, "I will give you a question, but don't answer it yet. Think silently," can at times trick models into thinking deeper into the question you had asked!

AI-Assisted Coding

Now that we have learned about different types of prompting. These skills can be used using different AI-assisted coding tools such as GitHub Copilot, Cursor, Replit, and Lovable to generate quality code rapidly and with ease. Besides AI-assisted coding tools, you can also use these techniques against popular LLM AI models such as Perplexity, Gemini, and ChatGPT to achieve similar results.

This tool can interpret natural language inputs to generate complex code and programs. Please keep in mind that the quality of prompting is pivotal for generating the appropriate code in the language of your choice.

Besides code generation, you can use these AI-assisted tools for the following:

- **Code Completion**: An environment like Cursor offers an IDE interface that can help in completing code as you type. This helps in reducing errors and speeding up tasks.

- **Documentation**: AI could help create code-level documentation and create reverse analysis of code and create adequate technical documentation.

- **Debugging**: AI is great at debugging code. Besides the tool mentioned above, you can use tools like DeepCode and SinCode to analyze and debug your code.

- **Rapid Prototyping**: AI is great for creating minimum viable prototypes and setting up boilerplate functionality with ease and rapidness.

- **Getting NFR Recommendation**: Often, nonfunctional requirements, such as performance, vertical and horizontal scaling, query optimization, and security, are difficult to implement. With the correct prompting, NFR could be well incorporated into your program and code base.

Summary

In this chapter, we learned about the various ways we can create prompts so that the LLM can produce optimized and relevant code. The nine different ways of prompting also provided examples to appreciate and understand the prompt engineering better. In the subsequent chapters, we will use these techniques to generate the relevant code to build our travel web application.

CHAPTER 7

Designing a Travel Experience Website

Introduction

Before we begin the core coding aspects leveraging AI for building our web application, thehalftimewhistle.com, let us get a quick orientation of the website layout. This travel website provides a personal collection of travel experiences from around the globe. The website can be leveraged to learn about a place of interest with curated itineraries, getting intrigued with interesting facts, and getting insider details of do's and don'ts. This chapter explores the site's core structure and layout so that it will be easy for you to relate to the coding that follows in the next chapter.

Home Page: An Outlet to Unlimited Adventures

The home page focuses on a simple and clean layout that gives access to all travel content that the website offers with simple navigation. The website is designed in a manner to ensure users can reach any content in three to four clicks.

The home page has a content section that highlights the site vision, followed by visually appealing content blocks that represent continents (such as North America, Europe, Asia, Oceania) – the highest level in the content hierarchy. Besides the continent, there is also a block that highlights either an upcoming travel destination or the last visited place. The blocks have an image and text representing the continent or the place and are action-driven. Tapping on a continent would navigate the user to a continent-specific page.

CHAPTER 7   DESIGNING A TRAVEL EXPERIENCE WEBSITE

The layout is designed to be clutter-free and intuitive and inculcates the best design practices to ensure high user retention. The content on this page is served directly by the web page and is not dynamically driven from a database. Although this may require an update of the web page for future continent inclusion, this design ensures faster loading time and an overall great user experience as the user clicks on the URL.

Speed is as important to your web application as its aesthetic appearance. Studies have shown that a slower response to accessing a web application results in more clicks off. This is why it's important to use the right technology when developing your web application.

Layered Navigation: From Continents to Regions

When the user clicks on the continent, it takes the user to the next level of navigation. In this second web page, users can see all the regions that the user has explored or visited. The design pattern of the page is the same as the home page. This is also a static web page for faster loading of content, and in the future, if a new region requires inclusion, the web page must be modified. Please note that we make these pages static as the layout and regions in a continent are largely constant. The application uses Static Site

CHAPTER 7   DESIGNING A TRAVEL EXPERIENCE WEBSITE

Generation (SSG) to pre-build the pages to quickly serve them. Here are a few examples to illustrate the region concept.

- If the user selects **North America** as the continent from the home page, the region page would show "Northeast", "Mid-West", "West", "South Central", "Southeast", "Jamaica", and "Canada".

- Similarly, if the user selects **Europe** as the continent from the home page, the region page would show Italy, France, Monaco, England, and Iceland.

By keeping the design pattern the same as the home page, the navigation is easy and helps the user to narrow their choices from a broad continent to a particular region or a country. This hierarchical design not only brings clarity but also helps create a consistent design approach essential for easier navigation and user retention.

Destinations: Showcasing Individual Journeys

Once the user selects a region, the website provides the third layer with specific travel experiences from the selected region. This is the page where content is dynamically generated by pulling data from the MongoDB database.

Let us take an example to understand this better. From the home page, the user selects **North America**. From the region page, the user selects **North East.** Now the third layer will show the following:

CHAPTER 7   DESIGNING A TRAVEL EXPERIENCE WEBSITE

- Shenandoah National Park
- Acadia National Park
- Portsmouth, New Hampshire
- White Mountains
- Empire State Escapades: My Adventures Across New York
- Incredible New Jersey
- Finger Lakes, NY

Each of these places has a brief narrative about the experience and an image to go with. The block design is consistent on this third layer as well.

These are the three layers that the user can navigate to get access to any content on the website. This organization also helps people to reach the content they wish to see methodically and easily.

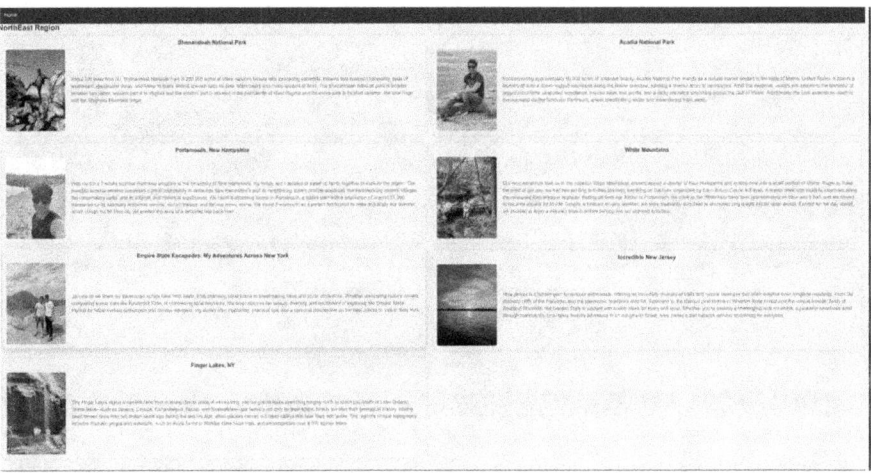

Schema Model

The following is the JSON data structure for our data model for this page (places.DB).

- **id**: This is the unique system-generated record ID.
- **description**: Short description of the place shown on the screen.
- **image**: Name of the image that is shown on the page (pulled from the CDN).

CHAPTER 7 DESIGNING A TRAVEL EXPERIENCE WEBSITE

- **region**: Region to which the place belongs (used for query).
- **title**: Title of the place shown on the page.

```
{
  "$schema": "https://json-schema.org/draft/2020-12/schema",
  "type": "object",
  "required": [
    "_id",
    "description",
    "image",
    "region",
    "title"
  ],
  "properties": {
    "_id": {
      "$ref": "#/$defs/ObjectId"
    },
    "description": {
      "type": "string"
    },
    "image": {
      "type": "string"
    },
    "region": {
      "type": "string"
    },
    "title": {
      "type": "string"
    }
  },
  "$defs": {
    "ObjectId": {
      "type": "object",
      "properties": {
        "$oid": {
```

91

```
              "type": "string",
              "pattern": "^[0-9a-fA-F]{24}$"
            }
          },
          "required": [
            "$oid"
          ],
          "additionalProperties": false
        }
      }
    }
```

Experience Pages: Deep Dives into Each Adventure

After the user has navigated to a particular experience, there are broadly two types of experience pages the user could see. The section below highlights it in detail.

Summary Experience Page

Let us understand the page design by taking an example from the website. From the home page, select **Europe,** and from the region page, select **Iceland**. This will bring you to the third layer with one option, **Seven Days Trip to Iceland. The page is rendered using Server Side Rendering (SSR) using Next.js to dynamically build the HTML based on user request. The content is fetched from MongoDB and rendered at the server side using SSR.** Selecting this option will provide you with the first type of experience page as described below:

- The page starts with a region title, Iceland Region, and a navigation link to take you back to the Iceland Region page.

- Next, you will see an image that represents the experience page with the title **Seven Days Trip to Iceland** shown under it.

- Below the main image is a scrolling image carousel that shows all the places visited in Iceland. Each of the images has a title that describes the place name. Clicking on the image will show the detailed experience page explained in the next section. In our example, the following places are shown:

- Blue Lagoon
- Georuberg Basalt Columns
- Ytri Tunga Seal Beach
- Búðir
- Arnarstapi
- Vatnshellir Cave Tour
- Saxhóll Crater
- Grundarfjörður
- Thingvellir National Park
- Geysir Hot Springs
- Reykjadalur Geothermal River
- Heimaey Island
- Snowmobile Tour – Mýrdalsjökull Glacier
- Ice-cave Glacier Hiking Tour
- Seljalandsfoss Waterfall
- Kopavogur dormant volcano
- Horseback Riding on Lava Fields
- Sky Lagoon
- Hallgrímskirkja Church

- Next, you will see a block of content providing a general overview of the plan and the itinerary.
- Following this blob of content is a section which provides a section on **interesting facts** about Iceland.
- The next section is about helpful tips to help plan your itinerary better.

CHAPTER 7   DESIGNING A TRAVEL EXPERIENCE WEBSITE

- A section dedicated to where we stayed.

- And then a day-wise summary of what we did – places visited, pictures, and images.

Detail Experience Page

When you click on any of the image carousels, a detailed description page providing all aspects of the place is displayed. In our example, we will tap on **Blue Lagoon**, the first experience in the image carousel. Please note that all images are stored in the GitHub CDN pages and accessed as a Statically.io CDN URL for faster access. The page will display the following:

- The page starts with a region title, **Iceland Region,** and a navigation link to take you back to the Seven Day Experience page

- Next, you will see an image that represents the experience with the title **Blue Lagoon** shown under it.

- The next block of content is **About the Place** – what is the place famous for and when did we visit the place.

- Next is **Our Experience** content block – in this block, you will find a free-flow text of the author's experience about the visited place, followed by a block of pictures.

- Next is a section on Interesting Facts from the place.

94

CHAPTER 7 DESIGNING A TRAVEL EXPERIENCE WEBSITE

- The section ends with a block of content on Other Details, which can have details like how to get there, what to bring, any price to pay to see the attraction, and the author's recommendation.

Please note that there are different experience pages based on the place visited. For example, a trail would also have sections like difficulty level, time required, and distance as some of the other content displayed.

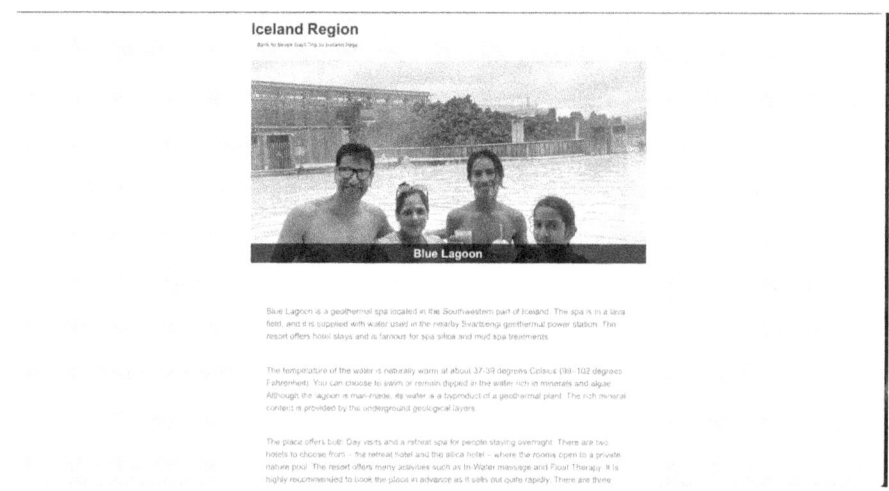

Schema Model

The following is the JSON data structure for our data model for this page (placedetails.DB):

- **id**: This is the unique system-generated record ID.
- **description**: Short description of the place shown on the screen.
- **image**: Name of the image that is shown on the page (pulled from the CDN).
- **region**: Region to which the place belongs (used for query).
- **title**: Title of the place shown on the page (also used for query).
- **commonBlocks**: Collection of repeating blocks of content with the following fields:
  - description

CHAPTER 7 DESIGNING A TRAVEL EXPERIENCE WEBSITE

- title

- days: A block with the following items, with description and a list of images

• **imageBlock**: For displaying the carousel (title and image name)

```
{
  "$schema": "https://json-schema.org/draft/2020-12/schema",
  "type": "object",
  "required": [
    "_id",
    "description",
    "image",
    "region",
    "title"
  ],
  "properties": {
    "_id": {
      "$ref": "#/$defs/ObjectId"
    },
    "commonBlocks": {
      "type": "array",
      "items": {
        "type": "object",
        "required": [
          "description",
          "title"
        ],
        "properties": {
          "description": {
            "type": "string"
          },
          "title": {
            "type": "string"
          }
```

```
          }
        }
      },
      "days": {
        "type": "array",
        "items": {
          "type": "object",
          "required": [
            "description"
          ],
          "properties": {
            "description": {
              "type": "string"
            },
            "images": {
              "type": "object",
              "required": [
                "0"
              ],
              "properties": {
                "0": {
                  "type": "string"
                },
                  —
              }
            },
            "title": {
              "type": "string"
            },
            "title": {
              "type": "string"
            }
          }
        }
      },
```

```
          "description": {
            "type": "string"
          },
          "image": {
            "type": "string"
          },
          "imageBlock": {
            "type": "array",
            "items": {
              "type": "object",
              "required": [
                "image",
                "title"
              ],
              "properties": {
                "image": {
                  "type": "string"
                },
                "title": {
                  "type": "string"
                }
              }
            }
          },
          "region": {
            "type": "string"
          },
          "title": {
            "type": "string"
          }
        },
        "$defs": {
          "ObjectId": {
            "type": "object",
            "properties": {
```

```
      "$oid": {
        "type": "string",
        "pattern": "^[0-9a-fA-F]{24}$"
      }
    },
    "required": [
      "$oid"
    ],
    "additionalProperties": false
  }
 }
}
```

Design Philosophy and User Experience

Thehalftimewhistle.com is designed with the following principles:

- Easy access to content – no content should take more than four clicks to reach.

- Cleaner design for easy consumption of data.

- Visually appealing site with easy and intuitive navigation.

- Responsive design so that the site renders on any device seamlessly, with a deep focus on user experience.

- Effectively address accessibility (a11y) and ARIA usage to enhance screen readability, regional user experience, and localization strategies.

- Build HTML elements such as headings with semantic structured content. This helps the screen readers to interpret the content and navigate with ease.

- Include a transcript for audio/video to support screen reader interaction.

- Use ARIA attributes to enhance form readability.

CHAPTER 7 DESIGNING A TRAVEL EXPERIENCE WEBSITE

Summary

This chapter provided the core concepts and design elements of the thehalftimewhistle.com website. Now that you have learned how the site is organized, we will dive into creating this web application in the next chapter.

CHAPTER 8

Application Configuration

Chapters 1 to 7 taught you the essential concepts required before you could create the web application. It provided you with a good appreciation of web application development, the choices of technologies we have made, and how AI could be used in building the same. We also discussed in greater detail various types of prompting you can use to get the desired result from various AI models.

With this background, let us now build our website www.thehalftimewhistle.com. In this chapter, we will explore the following concepts:

- Learn the core configuration work to ensure all technologies are working in harmony to produce the necessary results.

- Understand all front-end and back-end code configuration that will be required to make our website functional.

- Give examples of AI prompting so that you can relate to the type of prompting used and the subsequent results achieved.

- See the website as it gets built.

Environment Default System Files

When you install React.js and create your project, there are certain default files that get created, which are essential for managing project dependencies, metadata, build instructions, and environment-specific nuances. These files are essential for your application to function properly. In this section, we will learn about all such files.

CHAPTER 8   APPLICATION CONFIGURATION

package.json Configuration File

The package.json is the backbone of your project. It contains all the manifestations that are needed to organize the project and compile it accurately. Information such as project details, version of certain packages, and dependencies that your application needs to build are listed here. In our package.json file, we have the following:

- Information about our web application "thehalftimewhistle"
- All react scripts to start, build, and stop the application
- List of supporting browsers with version
- Node.js supported version

Let us break down the code and understand this better.

Did you know? As of 2025, there are around 2.5 million packages on npn! Package.json is simply one of them, but very important as it helps decide what packages are necessary for your personalized web application.

About the Project

```
{
  "name": "thehalftimewhistle",
  "version": "0.1.0",
  "private": true,
  "dependencies": {
    "@testing-library/jest-dom": "^5.17.0",
    "@testing-library/react": "^13.4.0",
    "@testing-library/user-event": "^13.5.0",
    "@vercel/analytics": "^1.3.2",
    "cors": "^2.8.5",
    "dompurify": "^3.1.7",
    "dotenv": "^16.4.5",
    "express": "^4.21.0",
    "mongoose": "^8.7.0",
```

```
    "react": "^18.3.1",
    "react-dom": "^18.3.1",
    "react-helmet": "^6.1.0",
    "react-router-dom": "^6.26.2",
    "react-scripts": "5.0.1",
    "web-vitals": "^2.1.4"
},
```

This JSON definition has all the relevant information about the project:

- **name**: Name of the project.

- **version**: Version of the project. This is user-defined.

- **private**: Flag to ensure the project is private and shouldn't be published to the public npm registry. If you are creating an open source project, setting this to public will make it ubiquitously available to all.

- **dependencies**: All the relevant dependent libraries are listed along with their version, which will make the application aware of key dependencies to avoid. Some key ones are mentioned below:

    - **react**: Core React libraries that render the user interface

    - **react-router-dom**: For helping with navigation

    - **react-helmet**: For SEO management

    - **mongoose**: For connecting with MongoDB, our back-end database

    - **web-vitals**: For Vercel web statistics measurement and reporting

React Scripts

```
"scripts": {
    "start": "react-scripts start",
    "build": "react-scripts build",
    "test": "react-scripts test",
```

```
    "eject": "react-scripts eject",
    "dev": "react-scripts start"
},
```

This part of the JSON code provides a script to run, compile, launch the test suite, perform eject to include all dependencies, and dev to start the development environment. Note that all these commands can be run on the command prompt using npm <script-name>. See explanation below:

- **start**: Runs the application.
- **build**: This command will compile the application and optimize the code.
- **test**: Launches the test runner to execute your test use cases.
- **eject**: This includes all dependencies in your project.json file so that you can customize it for specific needs.
- **dev**: Start the application in the development environment

ESLint Scripts

```
"eslintConfig": {
    "extends": [
        "react-app",
        "react-app/jest"
    ]
},
```

In React.js, Linting rules ensure code consistency and catch potential runtime errors, and Jest is the JavaScript testing framework.

The above line of code ensures you can directly mention eslint rules in this file instead of creating another config file.

Browser List

```
"browserslist": {
    "production": [
        ">0.2%",
```

```
      "not dead",
      "not op_mini all"
    ],
    "development": [
      "last 1 chrome version",
      "last 1 firefox version",
      "last 1 safari version"
    ]
  },
```

This code helps in defining the target browser that the application will support; based on this, different build tools (such as Babel) can generate optimized JavaScript and CSS for the specific browser support.

This way, by using different configurations, your code will be optimized to perform best in the choice of browser your user community uses.

Node.js Version Details

```
"engines": {
    "node": ">=18.18.0 <19.0.0"
  }
```

This tells the compiler which version of Node.js the application supports – this is important when you deploy the code on platforms such as Vercel, so that the right dependencies are called upon to avoid warning, error, and functionality issues.

Complete Code

Find below the complete code of package.json:

```
{
  "name": "thehalftimewhistle",
  "version": "0.1.0",
  "private": true,
  "dependencies": {
    "@testing-library/jest-dom": "^5.17.0",
    "@testing-library/react": "^13.4.0",
```

```
    "@testing-library/user-event": "^13.5.0",
    "@vercel/analytics": "^1.3.2",
    "cors": "^2.8.5",
    "dompurify": "^3.1.7",
    "dotenv": "^16.4.5",
    "express": "^4.21.0",
    "mongoose": "^8.7.0",
    "react": "^18.3.1",
    "react-dom": "^18.3.1",
    "react-helmet": "^6.1.0",
    "react-router-dom": "^6.26.2",
    "react-scripts": "5.0.1",
    "web-vitals": "^2.1.4"
  },
  "scripts": {
    "start": "react-scripts start",
    "build": "react-scripts build",
    "test": "react-scripts test",
    "eject": "react-scripts eject",
    "dev": "react-scripts start"
  },
  "eslintConfig": {
    "extends": [
      "react-app",
      "react-app/jest"
    ]
  },
  "browserslist": {
    "production": [
      ">0.2%",
      "not dead",
      "not op_mini all"
    ],
    "development": [
      "last 1 chrome version",
```

```
      "last 1 firefox version",
      "last 1 safari version"
    ]
  },
  "engines": {
    "node": ">=18.18.0 <19.0.0"
  }
}
```

package-lock.json

While package.json provides high-level dependencies, package-lock.json provides exact module-level dependencies so that every environment where this application will be deployed will exactly know which modules to call, what version to call, and what functionalities to achieve.

Unlike package.json, which could be manually managed, package-lock.json is system-generated and shouldn't be modified manually. We will not list the file here as it is a large file with over 19,000 lines. The following are some of the key features of this file:

- Create a complete **dependency tree**, creating an exact version for direct and their sub-dependencies.

- As you create your **CI/CD pipeline**, this guarantees version consistency, allowing your code to look identical across environments.

- When the dependencies are well defined, the **installation becomes faster** and error-free.

It is advisable to keep this file in version control to ensure a true copy of the latest package-lock.json is always available for reference.

Did you know? Package-lock-json was first introduced in 2017!

CHAPTER 8   APPLICATION CONFIGURATION

Before this, it was hard for tech devs to share their code with different developers. This is because the "npn install" command they would run, ran the latest compatible version. Each developer had slightly different versions, and the code couldn't work across the board.

server.js

In a full-stack application, server.js is the entry point of all server requests. Any HTTP requests made to the application are handled by server.js, and content is accordingly served to the end client. The following are some of the key functions of server.js:

- **Connecting to Back-End Databases:** Manages all incoming client requests, be it displaying content on a web page, API calls, database requests, or data processing.

- **Faster Access to React Files:** Access to static files created by React.js in the /build folder for faster access to web pages.

- **API Routing:** All API requests are securely handled and communicated with back-end servers.

- **Optimization:** It handles client-side rendering for faster access to content and optimizes SEO configuration for improved performance.

Over 30 million websites are powered by Node.js, with the majority having a server entry file like server.js!

Let us now understand our server.js configuration.

Environment, Imports, and App Setup

```
require('dotenv').config();
const mongoose = require('mongoose');
const express = require('express');
const cors = require('cors');
```

```
const path = require('path');
const app = express();
```

- require('dotenv').config();: Loads all necessary environment variables (e.g., database URL, port) from a .env file into process.env
- Imports core libraries:
  - mongoose: Used to interact with the MongoDB database for all location detail data.
  - express: Framework to build the HTTP server and API endpoints.
  - cors: Enables Cross-Origin Resource Sharing (CORS) for HTTP requests.
  - path: Utility for manipulating file and directory paths. All images are stored on the web server directly.
- const app = express();: Initializes the Express server instance

Middleware Setup

```
// Enable CORS for all routes
app.use(cors());
// Enable Mongoose debug mode
mongoose.set('debug', true);
```

- app.use(cors());: Allows all incoming HTTP requests from any origin. We will be using an API to get data from the back end, and this will help us enable the same. Developers should be aware that if the CORS permission settings are not set properly, it can expose sensitive data or back-end services to unauthorized sites. Access should be tightly controlled and properly audited to trust only trusted origins.
- mongoose.set('debug', true);: Enables debug logging for all MongoDB CRUD operations for easier debugging.

Static File Serving

```
// Serve static files from the React app
app.use(express.static(path.join(__dirname, 'build')));
```

- app.use(express.static(path.join(__dirname, 'build')));: Serves static files (the built React front end) located in the /build directory. This ensures faster rendering and higher performance.

MongoDB Connection

```
// MongoDB connection
const url = process.env.MONGODB_URI;
mongoose.connect(url, { useNewUrlParser: true, useUnifiedTopology: true })
  .then(() => console.log('Connected to MongoDB'))
  .catch(err => console.error('MongoDB connection error:', err));
```

- Reads the MongoDB URI from the environment variables (where all connection information is stored. You can get this info from your MongoDB console)
- Connects to MongoDB using Mongoose with modern connection options.
- Logs success or failure to the console.

MongoDB Schemas and Models

```
// Schema definition
const placeSchema = new mongoose.Schema({
  title: String,
  description: String,
  image: String
}, { strict: false });
// Model definition
const Place = mongoose.model('Place', placeSchema, 'places');
// Route handler for fetching specific place details by region and title
```

```
const placeDetailsSchema = new mongoose.Schema({
  place: String,
  title: String,
  days: [{
    title: String,
    description: String,
    images: [String]
  }],
  commonBlocks: [{
    title: String,
    description: String
  }]
}, { strict: false });
// Model definition for place details
const PlaceDetails = mongoose.model('PlaceDetails', placeDetailsSchema, 'placedetails');
```

Place Schema and Model

- This schema holds all the core places that the travel site will display.
- Schema: Defines a data structure for a place with a title, description, and image.
- Model: Place model for interacting with the places collection in MongoDB.

Place Details Schema and Model

- This schema contains details of each visited place.
- Schema: Represents detailed info about a place, including an itinerary (days) and reusable content blocks (commonBlocks).
- Model: PlaceDetails corresponds to the placedetails collection.

Please note the term {strict:false}; this lets the schema know that the document could save fields that aren't defined as part of the schema. This is useful in our context as we will have pages with different datasets, and not all datasets will be uniform.

API Route Handlers

```
// Route handlers
app.get('/api/places/:region', async (req, res) => {
  try {
    const { region } = req.params;
    const places = await Place.find({ region: region }).lean().exec();
    res.json(places);
  } catch (error) {
    console.error('Error fetching places:', error);
    res.status(500).json({ message: 'Error fetching places', error: error.
    toString() });
  }
});
```

Fetch Places by Region

GET /api/places/:region: Responds with all places matching the provided region parameter (regions are high-level areas such as Northeast and Midwest or countries such as Japan and Canada)

```
// Additional route to check database connection and collection
app.get('/api/dbcheck', async (req, res) => {
  try {
    const collections = await mongoose.connection.db.listCollections().
    toArray();
    const collectionNames = collections.map(c => c.name);
    res.json({
      dbName: mongoose.connection.db.databaseName,
      collections: collectionNames,
      connectionState: mongoose.connection.readyState
    });
  } catch (error) {
    console.error('Error checking database:', error);
    res.status(500).json({ message: 'Error checking database', error:
    error.message });
  }
});
```

CHAPTER 8 APPLICATION CONFIGURATION

- GET /api/dbcheck: Returns database name, list of collections, and connection state. Useful for diagnostics or deployment checks.

```
const { param, validationResult } = require('express-validator');
app.get('/api/placedetails/:region/:title',
  // Sanitization and validation chain for route params
  [
    param('region')
      .trim()
      .escape()
      .matches(/^[a-zA-Z0-9_-]+$/).withMessage('Invalid region format'),
    param('title')
      .trim()
      .escape()
      .matches(/^[a-zA-Z0-9 _-]+$/).withMessage('Invalid title format')
  ],
  async (req, res) => {
    // Check validation errors
    const errors = validationResult(req);
    if (!errors.isEmpty()) {
      return res.status(400).json({ errors: errors.array() });
    }
    try {
      const { region, title } = req.params;
      const placeDetails = await PlaceDetails.findOne({
        region: region,
        title: title
      }).lean().exec();

      if (!placeDetails) {
        return res.status(404).json({ message: 'Place details not found' });
      }
      res.json(placeDetails);
    } catch (error) {
      res.status(500).json({ message: 'Server error' });
    }
  });
```

```
    if (!placeDetails) {
      return res.status(404).json({ message: 'Place details not found' });
    }
    console.log(`Place details for ${title} in ${region}:`, JSON.
    stringify(placeDetails, null, 2));
    res.json(placeDetails);
  } catch (error) {
    console.error('Error fetching place details:', error);
    res.status(500).json({ message: 'Error fetching place details', error:
    error.toString() });
  }
});
```

Fetch Place Details

- GET /api/placedetails/:region/:title: Fetches place details for a specific region and title. The code checks whether the parameters are accurate before calling the route handler. Within a region, a content can be uniquely identified by the combination of region and title. This API gets all place details accordingly.

- If the place is not found, it returns a 404 error.

```
// Catch-all route to serve React app
app.get('*', (req, res) => {
  res.sendFile(path.join(__dirname, 'build', 'index.html'));
});
```

app.get('*', ...): Any request not matching the above routes serves the React app's index.html. This enables client-side routing support in React.

Operational and Error Handling Features

```
// Memory usage logging
setInterval(() => {
  const used = process.memoryUsage();
  console.log(`Memory usage: ${Math.round(used.rss / 1024 / 1024 * 100) /
  100} MB`);
```

```
}, 60000);
const PORT = process.env.PORT || 3000;
app.listen(PORT, () => console.log(`Server running on port ${PORT}`));
// Error handling for uncaught exceptions
process.on('uncaughtException', (error) => {
  console.error('Uncaught Exception:', error);
  // Optionally, you can choose to exit the process here
  // process.exit(1);
});

// Error handling for unhandled promise rejections
process.on('unhandledRejection', (reason, promise) => {
  console.error('Unhandled Rejection at:', promise, 'reason:', reason);
  // Optionally, you can choose to exit the process here
  // process.exit(1);
});
```

- **Memory Usage Logging:** Logs memory usage every minute to the console – helpful for monitoring resource usage in production

- **Listening on Port:** Starts the server on the PORT value from the environment or defaults to 3000

- **Global Error Handlers:** Listens for uncaught exceptions and unhandled promise rejections, logging them for effective error diagnostics

Complete Code

```
require('dotenv').config();
const mongoose = require('mongoose');
const express = require('express');
const cors = require('cors');
const path = require('path');
const app = express();

// Enable CORS for all routes
```

CHAPTER 8   APPLICATION CONFIGURATION

```
app.use(cors());

// Enable Mongoose debug mode
mongoose.set('debug', true);

// Serve static files from the React app
app.use(express.static(path.join(__dirname, 'build')));

// MongoDB connection
const url = process.env.MONGODB_URI;
mongoose.connect(url, { useNewUrlParser: true, useUnifiedTopology: true })
  .then(() => console.log('Connected to MongoDB'))
  .catch(err => console.error('MongoDB connection error:', err));

// Schema definition
const placeSchema = new mongoose.Schema({
  title: String,
  description: String,
  image: String
}, { strict: false });

// Model definition
const Place = mongoose.model('Place', placeSchema, 'places');

// Route handlers
app.get('/api/places/:region', async (req, res) => {
  try {
    const { region } = req.params;
    const places = await Place.find({ region: region }).lean().exec();
    res.json(places);
  } catch (error) {
    console.error('Error fetching places:', error);
    res.status(500).json({ message: 'Error fetching places', error: error.
    toString() });
  }
});

// Additional route to check database connection and collection
app.get('/api/dbcheck', async (req, res) => {
```

CHAPTER 8   APPLICATION CONFIGURATION

```
  try {
    const collections = await mongoose.connection.db.listCollections().
    toArray();
    const collectionNames = collections.map(c => c.name);
    res.json({
      dbName: mongoose.connection.db.databaseName,
      collections: collectionNames,
      connectionState: mongoose.connection.readyState
    });
  } catch (error) {
    console.error('Error checking database:', error);
    res.status(500).json({ message: 'Error checking database', error:
    error.message });
  }
});

// Schema definitions for place details
const placeDetailsSchema = new mongoose.Schema({
  place: String,
  title: String,
  days: [{
    title: String,
    description: String,
    images: [String]
  }],
  commonBlocks: [{
    title: String,
    description: String
  }]
}, { strict: false });

// Model definition for place details
const PlaceDetails = mongoose.model('PlaceDetails', placeDetailsSchema,
'placedetails');

// Route handler for fetching specific place details by region and title
app.get('/api/placedetails/:region/:title', async (req, res) => {
```

CHAPTER 8   APPLICATION CONFIGURATION

```
    try {
      const { region, title } = req.params;
      const placeDetails = await PlaceDetails.findOne({
        region: region,
        title: title
      }).lean().exec();

      if (!placeDetails) {
        return res.status(404).json({ message: 'Place details not found' });
      }
      console.log(`Place details for ${title} in ${region}:`, JSON.
      stringify(placeDetails, null, 2));
      res.json(placeDetails);
    } catch (error) {
      console.error('Error fetching place details:', error);
      res.status(500).json({ message: 'Error fetching place details', error:
      error.toString() });
    }
});

// Catch-all route to serve React app
app.get('*', (req, res) => {
  res.sendFile(path.join(__dirname, 'build', 'index.html'));
});

// Memory usage logging
setInterval(() => {
  const used = process.memoryUsage();
  console.log(`Memory usage: ${Math.round(used.rss / 1024 / 1024 * 100) /
  100} MB`);
}, 60000);

const PORT = process.env.PORT || 3000;
app.listen(PORT, () => console.log(`Server running on port ${PORT}`));

// Error handling for uncaught exceptions
process.on('uncaughtException', (error) => {
  console.error('Uncaught Exception:', error);
```

```
  // Optionally, you can choose to exit the process here
  // process.exit(1);
});

// Error handling for unhandled promise rejections
process.on('unhandledRejection', (reason, promise) => {
  console.error('Unhandled Rejection at:', promise, 'reason:', reason);
  // Optionally, you can choose to exit the process here
  // process.exit(1);
});
```

Examples of AI Prompting

Let us take a couple of AI prompting examples to help generate the code we understood above. Please note, always review the code for errors and omissions.

Schema Generation

Prompt:

Write Mongoose schema and model definitions for a MongoDB-backed Node.js application that manages travel destinations ("places") and detailed itineraries ("place details").

I need:

1. **A Place Schema and Model:**

    - Collection name: places

    - Fields:

        - title: String, the name of the place.

        - description: String, a description of the place.

        - image: String, a URL or path to an image representing the place.

    - Use { strict: false } in the schema options.

CHAPTER 8   APPLICATION CONFIGURATION

2. **A PlaceDetails Schema and Model:**
   - Collection name: placedetails
   - Fields:
     - place: String, referring to the associated place.
     - title: String, the itinerary title or section heading.
     - days: an array of objects, each with:
       - title: String, the day's title or heading.
       - description: String, a brief for the day.
       - images: an array of strings (image URLs or paths).
     - commonBlocks: an array of objects, each with:
       - title: String.
       - description: String.
   - Use { strict: false } in the schema options.

For both, define the Mongoose models, and explicitly set the collection names as shown above. Write the code in valid JavaScript for a Node.js application.

As you can see, the instructions are clear and detailed for the AI model to create the right code for you.

```
// Schema definition
const placeSchema = new mongoose.Schema({
  title: String,
  description: String,
  image: String
}, { strict: false });

// Model definition
const Place = mongoose.model('Place', placeSchema, 'places');
// Schema definitions for place details
const placeDetailsSchema = new mongoose.Schema({
  place: String,
  title: String,
```

```
    days: [{
      title: String,
      description: String,
      images: [String]
    }],
    commonBlocks: [{
      title: String,
      description: String
    }]
}, { strict: false });

// Model definition for place details
const PlaceDetails = mongoose.model('PlaceDetails', placeDetailsSchema,
'placedetails');
```

Get Data from MongoDB Based on a Region and Title Input Attribute

Prompt:

I'm building a Node.js Express API for a travel web application using MongoDB and Mongoose. I have a `PlaceDetails` Mongoose model.

I want you to write an Express route handler for the following:

Endpoint: `GET /api/placedetails/:region/:title`

Purpose: Fetch details for a specific place, where `region` and `title` are provided as URL parameters.

Functionality:

- Extract `region` and `title` from `req.params`.

- Use Mongoose to find a single `PlaceDetails` document that matches both `region` and `title`.

- Use `.lean().exec()` to return a plain JS object.

- If no matching document is found, return HTTP 404 and a JSON message saying, "Place details not found".

- If found, log the fetched place details to the console (nicely formatted with `JSON.stringify`).

CHAPTER 8   APPLICATION CONFIGURATION

- Respond with the place details as JSON.
- If there's an error, log the error and respond with HTTP 500 and an error message.
- Please provide the handler code, assuming the model `PlaceDetails` is already imported, and that `app` is an Express instance. Use async/await.

As you can see, knowledge of React is important to create the prompt with accuracy.

```
/ Route handler for fetching specific place details by region and title
app.get('/api/placedetails/:region/:title', async (req, res) => {
  try {
    const { region, title } = req.params;
    const placeDetails = await PlaceDetails.findOne({
      region: region,
      title: title
    }).lean().exec();

    if (!placeDetails) {
      return res.status(404).json({ message: 'Place details not found' });
    }
    console.log(`Place details for ${title} in ${region}:`, JSON.stringify(placeDetails, null, 2));
    res.json(placeDetails);
  } catch (error) {
    console.error('Error fetching place details:', error);
    res.status(500).json({ message: 'Error fetching place details', error: error.toString() });
  }
});
```

vercel.json

In our example, our target web server is Vercel. Vercel is a cloud platform that is widely popular for deploying and scaling serverless applications. Because of its ease of use, simple integration, and speed, it is quite popular in deploying front-end applications like ours.

Vercel.json files contain all the configuration files that will instruct Vercel about your environment; deployment specifications; any rewrites, redirects, and routing; image optimization; and schema validation.

Did you know? Vercel deploys thousands of apps per second! Vercel.json is the road map that tells Vercel about your app and its features.

```
{
  "rewrites": [
    { "source": "/api/places/:region", "destination": "/api/places/[region]" },
    { "source": "/api/placedetails/:region/:title", "destination": "/api/placedetails/[region]/[title]" },
    { "source": "/api/:path*", "destination": "/api/:path*" },
    { "source": "/(.*)", "destination": "/index.html" }
  ]
}
```

In this file, we have a series of rewrites. Rewrite is a routing rule that dynamically replaces the URL endpoint in Vercel without changing the user-visible URL. Here is a line-by-line explanation:

- When a request comes in like /api/places/northeast, Vercel rewrites it internally to /api/places/[region] and provides region as a parameter (region= northeast).

- If the user requests /api/placedetails/northeast/newjersey, Vercel maps it to /api/placedetails/[region]/[title] with parameters region= northeast, title= newjersey.

CHAPTER 8   APPLICATION CONFIGURATION

The above two URL definitions are important to fetch the relevant content from the database based on the content the user selects. Based on this URL, the correct API gets called to retrieve the values based on user selection:

- For any other /api/ request (not matched above), pass it through unchanged.

- Any other request (any URL path), serve the index.html file. This makes sure the user gets a page instead of a blank screen or an error.

App.js

App.js is a React default main entry component used for routing to different pages in an application. No navigation would work if you do not configure this file properly. The file uses **React Router** for client-side routing, which allows the app to display different pages based on the URL request made by the user. Let us understand the content of this file.

Imports

This section imports all the relevant libraries to enable navigation:

```
import React from 'react';
import { BrowserRouter as Router, Route, Routes } from 'react-router-dom';
import HomePage from './components/HomePage';
import Americas from "./components/NorthAmerica"
import Region from './components/Region'
import Europe from "./components/Europe"
import Asia from "./components/Asia"
import ContentDisplayOne from "./components/ContentDisplayOne"
import CentralAmerica from './components/CentralAmerica';
import Oceania from './components/Oceania';
import { Analytics } from "@vercel/analytics/react"
```

Broadly, there are either system-specific or application-specific imports.

- **React**: This is the core React library required for React-related functions.

- **BrowserRouter, Route, Routes:** These libraries enable navigation between "pages" without a full reload.

- **Component Imports:** Our application has multiple components, such as the home page, a page on a particular continent (North America, Europe, Asia, or Central America), and pages for displaying the region (Region) and the detailed content of the region (ContentDisplayOne). Any time you add a new page, that component is required to be imported here.

- **Analytics**: This is for Vercel (hosting provider) to track how users interact with our app for the purposes of metrics and analysis.

The App Component and Routing Breakdown

This is the function that will help in routing based on the URL request made by the user:

```
function App() {
  return (
    <Router>
      <div className="App">
        <Routes>
          <Route path="/" element={<HomePage />} />
          <Route path="/northamerica" element={<Americas />} />
          <Route path='/region' element={<Region />} />
          <Route path="/europe" element={<Europe />} />
          <Route path="/asia" element={<Asia />} />
          <Route path="/centralamerica" element={<CentralAmerica />} />
          <Route path="/oceania" element={<Oceania />} />

          <Route path="/content-display-one/*"
            element={<ContentDisplayOne />} />
          <Route path="/content-display-one/:region/:title"
            element={<ContentDisplayOne />} />
        </Routes>
        <Analytics />
```

```
        </div>
      </Router>
  );
}
export default App;
```

Let us first understand the key sections of the app:

- **<Router>:** Provides the app with the context of what needs to be routed.

- **<div className="App">:** A wrapper for styling.

- **<Routes>:** Wraps all possible routes (like a switch-case statement). Any new route must be mentioned here.

- **<Analytics />:** Adds Vercel analytics tracking to every page.

Some other key considerations:

- There are many continent-specific static pages where the routing is straightforward (Americas, Asia, Oceania, Europe).

- **/content-display-one/:region/:title** uses URL parameters (e.g., /content-display-one/Asia/India), which the ContentDisplayOne JS file can access and render data accordingly. The parameters are used to determine what content to retrieve from the back-end database.

- Two similar routes /contentdisplayone vs. /content-display-one (with and without a dash). This helps with flexible URLs and backward compatibility.

- Placing <Analytics /> at the root level means every page visit will be tracked. This is from Vercel and is used for collecting statistics about usage and visits.

Complete Code

Here is the complete code of app.js for your reference:

```
import React from 'react';
```

```jsx
import { BrowserRouter as Router, Route, Routes } from 'react-router-dom';
import HomePage from './components/HomePage';
import Americas from "./components/NorthAmerica"
import Region from './components/Region'
import Europe from "./components/Europe"
import Asia from "./components/Asia"
import ContentDisplayOne from "./components/ContentDisplayOne"
import CentralAmerica from './components/CentralAmerica';
import Oceania from './components/Oceania';
import { Analytics } from "@vercel/analytics/react"

function App() {
  return (
    <Router>
      <div className="App">
        <Routes>
          <Route path="/" element={<HomePage />} />
          <Route path="/northamerica" element={<Americas />} />
          <Route path='/region' element={<Region />} />
          <Route path="/europe" element={<Europe />} />
          <Route path="/asia" element={<Asia />} />
          <Route path="/centralamerica" element={<CentralAmerica />} />
          <Route path="/oceania" element={<Oceania />} />
          <Route path="/contentdisplayone"
            element={<ContentDisplayOne />} />
          <Route path="/content-display-one/*"
            element={<ContentDisplayOne />} />
          <Route path="/content-display-one/:region/:title"
            element={<ContentDisplayOne />} />
        </Routes>
        <Analytics />
      </div>
    </Router>
  );
}

export default App;
```

CHAPTER 8   APPLICATION CONFIGURATION

Example of AI Prompting
Generating MongoDB API Code

Prompt:

I'm building a React application using React Router v6 or above (with `react-router-dom`). I have a page component `ContentDisplayOne`.

Write a route definition that will render the `ContentDisplayOne` component when the user navigates to a path of the form `/content-display-one/:region/:title`, where `:region` and `:title` are dynamic URL parameters—for example, `/content-display-one/asia/japan`.

Requirements:

- Use the `<Route>` element from `react-router-dom`.

- The route path should be `/content-display-one/:region/:title`, with `region` and `title` being URL variables.

- The component displayed for this path should be `<ContentDisplayOne />`.

- Show only the route element code, as it would appear inside a `<Routes>` block.

- I want to be able to access the `region` and `title` parameters from inside `ContentDisplayOne` using React Router's hooks (like `useParams`).

```
<Route path="/content-display-one/:region/:title" element={<ContentDisplayOne />} />
```

Summary

In this chapter, we learned all the configuration files that are required to ensure our React application functions properly. We learned that some configuration files are system-generated files, and some are user-generated ones, required for the correct functioning of the app. We also learned about AI prompting through some real examples.

In our next chapter, we will build our homepage.

CHAPTER 9

The Landing Page: HomePage.js

Now that we have learned about all the configuration elements of our travel web application, let us start building the website. The first page the user would visit is the home page. Let us first have a quick look at how our page would look.

The page has the following components:

- The header image with a title
- A blurb of text providing a brief about the website
- Six clickable divs with images and text that represent a continent (except the first one, which highlights an upcoming attraction)
- And a footer highlighting copyright information

CHAPTER 9   THE LANDING PAGE: HOMEPAGE.JS

Let us now build this page.

When a user first clicks on your web app, they usually make an impression in just 50 milliseconds! This is why having a good starter page is important.

Import Statements

All the required system and functional imports are mentioned in this section.

```
import React from 'react';
import { Helmet } from 'react-helmet-async';
import { Link } from 'react-router-dom';
import './HomePage.css';

// Import images in multiple sizes for responsiveness
import BannerImageSmall from '../assets/banner-small.jpg';
import BannerImageMedium from '../assets/banner-medium.jpg';
import BannerImageLarge from '../assets/banner-large.jpg';

import NorthAmericaSmall from '../assets/northamerica-small.jpg';
import NorthAmericaMedium from '../assets/northamerica-medium.jpg';
import NorthAmericaLarge from '../assets/northamerica-large.jpg';

import CentralAmericaSmall from '../assets/centralamerica-small.jpg';
import CentralAmericaMedium from '../assets/centralamerica-medium.jpg';
import CentralAmericaLarge from '../assets/centralamerica-large.jpg';

import EuropeSmall from '../assets/europe-small.jpg';
import EuropeMedium from '../assets/europe-medium.jpg';
import EuropeLarge from '../assets/europe-large.jpg';

import AsiaSmall from '../assets/asia-small.jpg';
import AsiaMedium from '../assets/asia-medium.jpg';
import AsiaLarge from '../assets/asia-large.jpg';

import OceaniaSmall from '../assets/oceania-small.jpg';
import OceaniaMedium from '../assets/oceania-medium.jpg';
```

```
import OceaniaLarge from '../assets/oceania-large.jpg';

// Array of continent objects for easy mapping with images in different
sizes for responsiveness

const continents = [
  {
    name: "North America",
    images: { small: NorthAmericaSmall, medium: NorthAmericaMedium, large:
    NorthAmericaLarge }
  },
  {
    name: "Central America",
    images: { small: CentralAmericaSmall, medium: CentralAmericaMedium,
    large: CentralAmericaLarge }
  },
  {
    name: "Europe",
    images: { small: EuropeSmall, medium: EuropeMedium, large:
    EuropeLarge }
  },
  {
    name: "Asia",
    images: { small: AsiaSmall, medium: AsiaMedium, large: AsiaLarge }
  },
  {
    name: "Oceania",
    images: { small: OceaniaSmall, medium: OceaniaMedium, large:
    OceaniaLarge }
  },
];
```

System Imports

- **React**: Required for React component functions.
- **Helmet**: This package helps in getting the HTML <head> with details for SEO tracking enablement.

- **Link, useNavigate**: Helps to navigate to a page without reloading the entire page.

Functional Imports

- **HomePage.css**: This is a custom CSS file for all stylesheets and page design (we will explore this file soon).
- **banner**: Importing images for the top image on the page.
- **Continent Images**: All the div tag images for the continent.

Continent Object

- Create a single array (continents) to store all continent names for easy access and practice creating clean code.

Page Navigation

Ensuring you have good navigation features on the first page is very important. It should be clear to the user where they need to go and how to get to their destination easily.

This section has the code to navigate to the different continents as the user clicks on the displayed divs.

```
const HomePage = () => {
  const navigate = useNavigate();
  const handleBlockClick = (destination) => {
    navigate(`/${destination.toLowerCase()}`);
};
```

- HomePage is a React functional component.
- useNavigate: Allows for programmatic navigation by calling this function.

- handleBlockClick: When the user clicks a continent block, it navigates to a new route like /northamerica, /europe, etc. Please note that it takes the destination as an input. This allows the future addition of a continent easy.

Managing Meta Data and SEO

The following enables SEO inclusion for making search engines find our site easily.

```
<Helmet>
    <title>The Half Time Travel Website - Family Travel
    Adventures</title>
    <meta
      name="description"
      content="Explore family travel adventures, itineraries, and off-
      the-beaten-path experiences across continents. Plan your next
      journey with The Half Time Travel Website."
    />
    <meta
      property="og:title"
      content="The Half Time Travel Website - Family Travel Adventures"
    />
    <meta
      property="og:description"
      content="Discover unique family travel experiences and
      itineraries across continents. Plan your next adventure with The
      Half Time Travel Website."
    />
    <meta
      property="og:image"
      content={BannerImageLarge}
    />
    <script type="application/ld+json">
      {JSON.stringify({
        "@context": "https://schema.org",
```

```
            "@type": "TravelBlog",
            name: "The Half Time Travel Website",
            description: "Family travel adventures and itineraries across
            continents",
            url: "https://www.thehalftimewhistle.com",
            image: BannerImageLarge,
        })}
    </script>
</Helmet>
```

Helmet helps in pushing everything mentioned within <helmet> for SEO consideration. In our example, we have a title, description, image, and certain metadata. This will help our travel site to be easily indexed by search engines such as Google.

Main Page Layout

Let us now go through the page layout code:

```
<div className="home-page">
```

React.js allows HTML code to co-mingle with JavaScript. This is the div tag of our HTML page. The class name we will see in our CSS file, which will help in designing the div (you will see it in the next section).

```
<header className="header">
        <nav className="nav-menu">
          <ul className="menu-level-1">
            <li><Link to="/">Home</Link></li>
          </ul>
        </nav>
        <div className="banner">
          <img
            src={BannerImageLarge}
            srcSet={`${BannerImageSmall} 480w, ${BannerImageMedium} 800w,
            ${BannerImageLarge} 1200w`}
            sizes="(max-width: 600px) 480px, (max-width: 960px)
            800px, 1200px"
```

```
            alt="The Half Time Travel Website Banner"
            className="banner-image"
            loading="lazy"
        />              <h1 className="banner-text">Welcome to The Half
                        Time Travel Website</h1>
    </div>
</header>
```

The header includes the banner image and a navigation menu (single-item menu with title "Home"). Notice the loading of the image is lazy, which helps in faster loading of the page, as the page wouldn't wait for the image to load to display the rest of the content.

```
<main className="main-content">
```

This is the main section, which will contain the text blurb and our six blocks of div for continents.

```
<section className="common-block">
            <h2>Our Family Travel Philosophy</h2>
            <p>We love to travel as a family—exploring new destinations,
            experiencing diverse cultures, and embracing the life of true
            wanderers. When we plan a trip, the process of creating the
            itinerary is often a daunting task. We prefer to explore like
            locals—renting cars, staying in Airbnbs, and stepping off the
            beaten path.</p>
            <p>For a long time, I've wanted to create a log of all our
            travel experiences in one place—a space that not only serves
            as our family travelogue, allowing us to relive our cherished
            memories, but also as a resource for others. We hope that
            people will read about our adventures and, perhaps, feel
            inspired to visit some of the places we've been.</p>
            <h3>Why "Half Time Whistle"?</h3>
            <p>In any game, a whistle signals a break—a time to refuel,
            rejuvenate, and rethink. Our Half Time Whistle website is
            inspired by this concept, encouraging you to take a pause
            from your busy life to wander, explore, and rediscover the
            world.</p>
```

CHAPTER 9   THE LANDING PAGE: HOMEPAGE.JS

```
            <p>Half Time Whistle is not just a travel website; it's a piece
            of our heart and soul. It's a collection of our memories, woven
            together with passion and love. We hope you enjoy this space as
            much as we enjoy creating and nurturing it.</p>
            <p>Shantanu, Kapila, Shaurya, and Nitara</p>
        </section>
```

This is the first section under the main section that displays the text blurb as HTML content.

```
<section className="content-blocks">
            <article className="block featured-block">
              <div className="star-icon" aria-hidden="true">★</div>
              <div className="block-content">
<img
                src={BannerImageLarge}
                srcSet={`${BannerImageSmall} 480w, ${BannerImageMedium} 800w, ${BannerImageLarge} 1200w`}
                sizes="(max-width: 600px) 480px, (max-width: 960px) 800px, 1200px"
                alt="Smoky Mountains National Park"
                loading="lazy"
              />              <h2>Coming Up - Smoky Mountains National
                                Park - Nov'24</h2>
              </div>
            </article>
//Continent Block with links
            {continents.map(continent => (
            <Link
              key={continent.name}
              to={`/${continent.name.replace(/\s+/g, '')}`}
              className="block"
            >
              <article className="block-content">
                <img
                  src={continent.image}
```

```
              alt={`${continent.name} Travel Destinations`}
              loading="lazy"
            />
            <h2>{continent.name}</h2>
          </article>
        </Link>
      ))}
    </section>
  </main>
```

This is the second section that displays the continent blocks. Each block demonstrates the following function:

- Each <article className="block"> represents a clickable region (in our parlance continent).
- onClick handler navigates to the correct continent page.
- Recall we have a function that handles navigation based on the title input. As you can see, each click passes the correct continent name as input. Each of the continents has a page, which we will understand in the subsequent chapters.
- Each image uses srcSet and size attributes for responsive loading.
- Imported multiple image sizes for banner and continent images.
- The browser will pick the optimal image based on device viewport width.
- Accessibility is preserved with meaningful alt texts.
- Maintained semantic structure with <Link> wrapping <article> blocks for continent navigation.

```
<footer className="footer">
    <p>&copy; 2024 TheHalfTimeTravel and TheHalfTimeWhistle Website.
    All rights reserved.</p>
    <p>Disclaimer: All images and content are our personal opinion
    and should be read and viewed from that perspective</p>
</footer>
```

This is the footer that displays the copyright and disclaimers.

Complete Code

```
import React from 'react';
import { Helmet } from 'react-helmet-async';
import { Link } from 'react-router-dom';
import './HomePage.css';

// Import images in multiple sizes for responsiveness
import BannerImageSmall from '../assets/banner-small.jpg';
import BannerImageMedium from '../assets/banner-medium.jpg';
import BannerImageLarge from '../assets/banner-large.jpg';

import NorthAmericaSmall from '../assets/northamerica-small.jpg';
import NorthAmericaMedium from '../assets/northamerica-medium.jpg';
import NorthAmericaLarge from '../assets/northamerica-large.jpg';

import CentralAmericaSmall from '../assets/centralamerica-small.jpg';
import CentralAmericaMedium from '../assets/centralamerica-medium.jpg';
import CentralAmericaLarge from '../assets/centralamerica-large.jpg';

import EuropeSmall from '../assets/europe-small.jpg';
import EuropeMedium from '../assets/europe-medium.jpg';
import EuropeLarge from '../assets/europe-large.jpg';

import AsiaSmall from '../assets/asia-small.jpg';
import AsiaMedium from '../assets/asia-medium.jpg';
import AsiaLarge from '../assets/asia-large.jpg';

import OceaniaSmall from '../assets/oceania-small.jpg';
import OceaniaMedium from '../assets/oceania-medium.jpg';
import OceaniaLarge from '../assets/oceania-large.jpg';

// Array of continent objects for easy mapping with images in different sizes for responsiveness
const continents = [
  {
```

```
    name: "North America",
    images: { small: NorthAmericaSmall, medium: NorthAmericaMedium, large:
    NorthAmericaLarge }
  },
  {
    name: "Central America",
    images: { small: CentralAmericaSmall, medium: CentralAmericaMedium,
    large: CentralAmericaLarge }
  },
  {
    name: "Europe",
    images: { small: EuropeSmall, medium: EuropeMedium, large:
    EuropeLarge }
  },
  {
    name: "Asia",
    images: { small: AsiaSmall, medium: AsiaMedium, large: AsiaLarge }
  },
  {
    name: "Oceania",
    images: { small: OceaniaSmall, medium: OceaniaMedium, large:
    OceaniaLarge }
  },
];

const HomePage = () => {
  return (
    <>
      <Helmet>
        <title>The Half Time Travel Website - Family Travel
        Adventures</title>
        <meta
          name="description"
          content="Explore family travel adventures, itineraries, and off-
          the-beaten-path experiences across continents. Plan your next
          journey with The Half Time Travel Website."
```

```jsx
          />
          <meta
            property="og:title"
            content="The Half Time Travel Website - Family Travel Adventures"
          />
          <meta
            property="og:description"
            content="Discover unique family travel experiences and
            itineraries across continents. Plan your next adventure with The
            Half Time Travel Website."
          />
          <meta
            property="og:image"
            content={BannerImageLarge}
          />
          <script type="application/ld+json">
            {JSON.stringify({
              "@context": "https://schema.org",
              "@type": "TravelBlog",
              name: "The Half Time Travel Website",
              description: "Family travel adventures and itineraries across
              continents",
              url: "https://www.thehalftimewhistle.com",
              image: BannerImageLarge,
            })}
          </script>
      </Helmet>

      <div className="home-page">
        <header className="header">
          <nav className="nav-menu">
            <ul className="menu-level-1">
              <li><Link to="/">Home</Link></li>
            </ul>
          </nav>
          <div className="banner">
```

```
    <img
      src={BannerImageLarge}
      srcSet={`${BannerImageSmall} 480w, ${BannerImageMedium} 800w,
      ${BannerImageLarge} 1200w`}
      sizes="(max-width: 600px) 480px, (max-width: 960px)
      800px, 1200px"
      alt="The Half Time Travel Website Banner"
      className="banner-image"
      loading="lazy"
    />
    <h1 className="banner-text">Welcome to The Half Time Travel
    Website</h1>
  </div>
</header>

<main className="main-content">
  <section className="common-block">
    <h2>Our Family Travel Philosophy</h2>
    <p>We love to travel as a family—exploring new destinations,
    experiencing diverse cultures, and embracing the life of true
    wanderers. When we plan a trip, the process of creating the
    itinerary is often a daunting task. We prefer to explore like
    locals—renting cars, staying in Airbnbs, and stepping off the
    beaten path.</p>
    <p>For a long time, I've wanted to create a log of all our
    travel experiences in one place—a space that not only serves
    as our family travelogue, allowing us to relive our cherished
    memories, but also as a resource for others. We hope that
    people will read about our adventures and, perhaps, feel
    inspired to visit some of the places we've been.</p>
    <h3>Why "Half Time Whistle"?</h3>
    <p>In any game, a whistle signals a break—a time to refuel,
    rejuvenate, and rethink. Our Half Time Whistle website is
    inspired by this concept, encouraging you to take a pause
    from your busy life to wander, explore, and rediscover the
    world.</p>
```

```
      <p>Half Time Whistle is not just a travel website; it's a piece
      of our heart and soul. It's a collection of our memories, woven
      together with passion and love. We hope you enjoy this space as
      much as we enjoy creating and nurturing it.</p>
      <p>Shantanu, Kapila, Shaurya, and Nitara</p>
    </section>

    <section className="content-blocks">
      {/* Featured Static Block */}
      <article className="block featured-block">
        <div className="star-icon" aria-hidden="true">★</div>
        <div className="block-content">
          <img
            src={BannerImageLarge}
            srcSet={`${BannerImageSmall} 480w, ${BannerImageMedium}
            800w, ${BannerImageLarge} 1200w`}
            sizes="(max-width: 600px) 480px, (max-width: 960px)
            800px, 1200px"
            alt="Smoky Mountains National Park"
            loading="lazy"
          />
          <h2>Coming Up - Smoky Mountains National Park - Nov'24</h2>
        </div>
      </article>

      {/* Continent Blocks */}
      {continents.map(({ name, images }) => (
        <Link
          key={name}
          to={`/${name.replace(/\s+/g, '')}`}
          className="block"
        >
          <article className="block-content">
            <img
              src={images.large}
```

```
              srcSet={`${images.small} 480w, ${images.medium} 800w,
              ${images.large} 1200w`}
              sizes="(max-width: 600px) 480px, (max-width: 960px)
              800px, 1200px"
              alt={`${name} Travel Destinations`}
              loading="lazy"
            />
            <h2>{name}</h2>
          </article>
        </Link>
      ))}
      </section>
    </main>

    <footer className="footer">
      <p>&copy; 2024 TheHalfTimeTravel and TheHalfTimeWhistle Website.
      All rights reserved.</p>
      <p>Disclaimer: All images and content are our personal opinion
      and should be read and viewed from that perspective</p>
    </footer>
   </div>
  </ />
 );
};

export default HomePage;
```

AI Prompting

Let us now create a prompt that can create the home page for us from an AI LLM. Please note, always review the code for errors and omissions.

Prompt

I want you to generate a complete functional React component for the home page of a travel application called "The Half Time Travel Website".

The requirements are:

Tech stack:

Use React functional components.

Use `react-router-dom`'s `Link` and `useNavigate` for navigation.

Use `react-helmet` to set SEO meta tags (title, description, Open Graph, and JSON-LD structured data).

Import images for: a top banner, and for five continent blocks (North America, Central America, Europe, Asia, Oceania) from an `assets` directory.

Import a local CSS file for styling.

Layout/Sections Required:

A container `<div>` with class `home-page`.

Header:

Simple nav bar with a "Home" link.

Banner image with alt text.

Main title welcoming users.

Main content:

Section with a short "Family Travel Philosophy" including a heading, some paragraphs ("<text to include>"), and a subheading "Why 'Half Time Whistle'?" with explanation as per the content below "<include text>"

Section with blocks for each continent (North America, Central America, Europe, Asia, Oceania). Each block should:

Display an image and the continent name.

On click, use `useNavigate` to go to `/<continent>`, lowercased (e.g., `/northamerica`).

One "featured" block at the top of this section, with a star icon, an image, and the text "Coming Up - Smoky Mountains National Park - Nov'24".

Footer:

Use the following text "<include text>"

Accessibility and Best Practices:

All images must have descriptive `alt` attributes.

Images should use `loading="lazy"`.

Use semantic HTML (e.g., `<header>`, `<main>`, `<footer>`, `<section>`, `<article>`).

Add `aria-hidden="true"` on decorative icons.

Meta Data for Helmet:

Set appropriate `<title>`, `<meta name="description">`.

Open Graph tags: `og:title`, `og:description`, `og:image`.

Add a JSON-LD travel blog schema script, with the blog name, description, canonical URL, and banner image.

Other:

Export the component as default.

No TypeScript – plain JS.

Include class names for CSS, but do not generate CSS yet

Use placeholder or variable names for the imports (`banner`, `northamerica`, etc.).

Please write clear, commented, readable code.

Output only the code file.

Why Does This Prompt Work?

Context and Branding: Gives the site name and some narrative for the family/travel focus.

Structure: Explicitly specifies components, block arrangement, and which technologies to use.

Navigation: Details the logic for the continent blocks and their navigation.

SEO: Instructs the model to use react-helmet with rich metadata.

Accessibility: Requests proper alt attributes, lazy loading, semantic HTML, and ARIA where needed.

Clarity for Output: Tells the AI not to add anything but the code (no prose, explanations).

Adjusting for Even Higher Accuracy

Add Example Data: Provide your own write-up. Although we can ask the AI to write, we would like to write on our own.

Prefer Snippet-Only: Always instruct the AI to "output code only" to cut out explanations.

Home Page Stylesheet

We will learn in this section how to style the page we just created.

CHAPTER 9   THE LANDING PAGE: HOMEPAGE.JS

Overarching Layout

```
.home-page {
  font-family: Arial, sans-serif;
  display: flex;
  flex-direction: column;
  min-height: 100vh;
}
```

Three critical things are defined in this style, which is applied to the entire home page:

- Applies Arial font to all text.
- Uses flexbox in a column, so header, main, and footer stack vertically.
- Ensures the page is at least the full height of the browser.

Header and Banner Layout

```
.header {
  position: relative;
}
.banner {
  position: relative;
}
```

Allows the banner and header text to be positioned relative to their parents.

Banner Image and Text

```
.banner-image {
  width: 100%;
  height: 300px;
  object-fit: cover;
}
.banner-text {
```

```
    position: absolute;
    top: 50%;
    left: 50%;
    transform: translate(-50%, -50%);
    color: white;
    font-size: 2.0em;
    text-shadow: 2px 2px 4px rgba(0,0,0,0.5);
}
```

- Banner image stretches to the full width, fixed height, cropping with object-fit: cover.
- Banner text is centered over the image, white, larger, with a drop shadow for readability.

Navigation Bar

```
.nav-menu {
  background-color: #333;
}
.menu-level-1 {
  list-style-type: none;
  margin: 0;
  padding: 0;
  display: flex;
}
.menu-level-1 > li {
  position: relative;
}
.menu-level-1 > li > a {
  display: block;
  color: white;
  text-align: center;
  padding: 14px 16px;
  text-decoration: none;
```

```
}
.menu-level-1 > li > a:hover {
  background-color: #111;
}
```

This is for the navigation menu on the top bar. The following are the key design elements applied to it:

- Dark navbar with horizontal links.
- Links become darker on hover.
- No bullet points, using flexbox for left-to-right arrangement.

Main Content Area

```
.main-content {
  flex: 1 0 auto;
}
```

This is where the text blurb and continent blocks will be displayed. In this, the design consideration is as below:

- Stretches the main content to take up available vertical space between the header and footer.

Content Block Design

```
.content-blocks {
  margin-top: 10px;
  display: grid;
  grid-template-columns: repeat(auto-fit, minmax(280px, 1fr));
  gap: 16px; /* space between grid items */
  justify-content: center; /* centers the grid container if not full width */
}
.block {
  width: 30%;
```

```
  margin-bottom: 20px;
  text-align: center;
  cursor: pointer;
}
.block-content {
  background-color: #f0f0f0;
  border-radius: 20px 20px 0 0;
  overflow: hidden;
  box-shadow: 0 4px 8px rgba(0,0,0,0.1);
  transition: transform 0.3s ease-in-out;
}
.block-content:hover {
  transform: translateY(-10px);
}
.block img {
  width: 100%;
  height: 200px;
  object-fit: cover;
}
```

These are the content blocks for the continent (except the first featured block). The design considerations are as follows:

- Arranges region blocks in a responsive row; wraps onto new lines if there's not enough space.

- Each block takes up ~1/3 of the width on large screens, spaced out, centered, and clickable.

- Rounded top corners, soft shadow, light background, pops up slightly on hover.

- Card moves up 10px on hover for a floating effect.

- Region images fully fill the card width and a fixed height, cropped as needed.

CHAPTER 9   THE LANDING PAGE: HOMEPAGE.JS

Featured Block Style

```css
/* Featured block styles */
.featured-block .block-content {
  background-color: #e0e0e0;
  border: 2px solid #007bff;
  box-shadow: 0 6px 12px rgba(0,0,0,0.15);
}
.featured-block p {
  color: #007bff;
}
/* Hover effects */
.block:hover {
  transform: translateY(-5px);
}
.featured-block:hover {
  transform: translateY(-5px) scale(1.05);
}
.featured-block {
  position: relative;
}
.star-icon {
  position: absolute;
  top: -10px;
  left: 50%;
  transform: translateX(-50%);
  background-color: #ffd700; /* Gold color for the star */
  color: #fff;
  font-size: 24px;
  width: 40px;
  height: 40px;
  display: flex;
  justify-content: center;
  align-items: center;
  border-radius: 50%;
  z-index: 1;
```

```
    box-shadow: 0 2px 4px rgba(0,0,0,0.2);
}
.featured-block .block-content {
    border-top: 3px solid #ffd700; /* Gold border to match the star */
    padding-top: 20px; /* Add some space for the star */
}
```

This is for the first block to display the featured place. Here are the design considerations:

- Slightly different color, thicker border, bigger shadow for the featured card.
- On hover, it lifts and slightly enlarges (scale (1.05)).
- The star icon for the featured block: gold circle with a white star, centered above the card, with a shadow.
- Top gold border and padding so the star doesn't overlap the card content.

Footer Design

```
.footer {
    background-color: #333;
    color: white;
    text-align: center;
    padding: 5px 0;
    flex-shrink: 0;
}
```

Footer sticks to the bottom (with flex layout), centered white text on dark background.

Media Queries: Responsive Design

```
@media (max-width: 768px) {
    .block {
```

```
      width: 45%;
    }
  }
  @media (max-width: 480px) {
    .block {
      width: 100%;
    }
  }
```

This is for laying out the site on different form factors. The following are the key considerations:

- **Medium Screens (≤768px)**: Blocks become two per row (45% width each).

- **Small Screens (≤480px)**: Each block is full-width (stacked vertically), making the site mobile-friendly.

Complete Code

```
.home-page {
  font-family: Arial, sans-serif;
  display: flex;
  flex-direction: column;
  min-height: 100vh;
}
.header {
  position: relative;
}
.banner {
  position: relative;
}
.banner-image {
  width: 100%;
  height: 300px;
  object-fit: cover;
```

```css
}
.banner-text {
  position: absolute;
  top: 50%;
  left: 50%;
  transform: translate(-50%, -50%);
  color: white;
  font-size: 2.0em;
  text-shadow: 2px 2px 4px rgba(0,0,0,0.5);
}
.nav-menu {
  background-color: #333;
}
.menu-level-1 {
  list-style-type: none;
  margin: 0;
  padding: 0;
  display: flex;
}
.menu-level-1 > li {
  position: relative;
}
.menu-level-1 > li > a {
  display: block;
  color: white;
  text-align: center;
  padding: 14px 16px;
  text-decoration: none;
}
.menu-level-1 > li > a:hover {
  background-color: #111;
}
.main-content {
  flex: 1 0 auto;
}
```

CHAPTER 9   THE LANDING PAGE: HOMEPAGE.JS

```css
.content-blocks {
  margin-top: 10px;
  display: grid;
  grid-template-columns: repeat(auto-fit, minmax(280px, 1fr));
  gap: 16px; /* space between grid items */
  justify-content: center; /* centers the grid container if not full width */
}
.block {
  width: 30%;
  margin-bottom: 20px;
  text-align: center;
  cursor: pointer;
}
.block-content {
  background-color: #f0f0f0;
  border-radius: 20px 20px 0 0;
  overflow: hidden;
  box-shadow: 0 4px 8px rgba(0,0,0,0.1);
  transition: transform 0.3s ease-in-out;
}
.block-content:hover {
  transform: translateY(-10px);
}
.block img {
  width: 100%;
  height: 200px;
  object-fit: cover;
}
/* Featured block styles */
.featured-block .block-content {
  background-color: #e0e0e0;
  border: 2px solid #007bff;
  box-shadow: 0 6px 12px rgba(0,0,0,0.15);
}
```

```css
.featured-block p {
  color: #007bff;
}
/* Hover effects */
.block:hover {
  transform: translateY(-5px);
}
.featured-block:hover {
  transform: translateY(-5px) scale(1.05);
}
.featured-block {
  position: relative;
}
.star-icon {
  position: absolute;
  top: -10px;
  left: 50%;
  transform: translateX(-50%);
  background-color: #ffd700; /* Gold color for the star */
  color: #fff;
  font-size: 24px;
  width: 40px;
  height: 40px;
  display: flex;
  justify-content: center;
  align-items: center;
  border-radius: 50%;
  z-index: 1;
  box-shadow: 0 2px 4px rgba(0,0,0,0.2);
}
.featured-block .block-content {
  border-top: 3px solid #ffd700; /* Gold border to match the star */
  padding-top: 20px; /* Add some space for the star */
}
.footer {
```

```
    background-color: #333;
    color: white;
    text-align: center;
    padding: 5px 0;
    flex-shrink: 0;
  }
  @media (max-width: 768px) {
    .block {
      width: 45%;
    }
  }
  @media (max-width: 480px) {
    .block {
      width: 100%;
    }
  }
```

Did you know? 75% of users base their web app's credibility on its design! This includes factors like the colors, font, and style you used.

AI Prompting

Let us now learn the AI prompt that will be required to generate the code. Please note that all AI output should be read and modified for errors and omissions.

Prompt for Generating This CSS

Write a complete CSS stylesheet for the homepage of a travel blog website, named `HomePage.css`. The CSS will support a modern, mobile-responsive React homepage with the following requirements and style details:

Overall Layout

- The root element has the class `.home-page`.

- Use a clean sans-serif font (Arial or similar) across the site.
- Use CSS Flexbox for vertical stacking: header at the top, main content in the middle (fills available space), footer at the bottom.
- Ensure the page takes at least the full viewport height (`min-height: 100vh`).

Header & Banner

- The header (`.header`) should allow absolutely positioned elements inside.
- The banner section (`.banner`) is relative. The banner image (`.banner-image`) covers full width, with a fixed height (300px) and uses `object-fit: cover` to crop appropriately.
- Add a `.banner-text` element absolutely centered over the image, with large white text (2em), and a drop shadow for visibility.

Navigation Bar

- The navigation menu (`.nav-menu`) is a horizontal bar with a dark background (#333).
- The top-level menu list (`.menu-level-1`) is a flex row, items are inline, no bullets.
- Menu links (`li > a`) are white, have centered text, good vertical padding, no underline, and a hover effect that darkens the background (#111).

Main Content

- `.main-content` should expand to fill available vertical space in the flex layout.

Content Blocks Layout

- `.content-blocks` uses `display: flex`, wraps if necessary, and spaces blocks evenly with `justify-content: space-around`, and a `margin-top` of 10px.
- Each `.block` is a card with:

- ~30% width on large screens.
- Centered text.
- 20px vertical margin.
- Pointer cursor on hover.

Block Card Style

- `.block-content` has:
  - Light gray background (`#f0f0f0`), rounded top corners.
  - Box shadow for a raised effect.
  - Transition so it floats up (`translateY(-10px)`) on hover.
- Images inside blocks (`.block img`) fill width, fixed 200px height, using `object-fit: cover`.

Featured Block

- `.featured-block .block-content` is visually distinct:
  - Slightly darker background (`#e0e0e0`), thick blue border (`#007bff`), larger shadow.
  - Top gold border (`#ffd700`) to match a star icon.
  - Extra top padding for the star.
- The featured block (`.featured-block`) is relative, and on hover it both lifts (`translateY(-5px)`) and gently enlarges (`scale(1.05)`).
- The `.star-icon` is:
  - Absolutely positioned above the card, centered.
  - Gold circle with a white star (font icon or emoji), with drop shadow, fixed size (40px by 40px), flex centered.
  - Any `<p>` inside the featured block is colored blue (`#007bff`).

Hover Effects

- All `.block` cards translate up slightly (-5px) on hover.
- Featured block does both translation and scaling for stronger effect.

Footer

- `.footer` is dark (#333), white text, centered, small vertical padding. It must stick to the bottom with the flex layout (`flex-shrink: 0`).

Responsive Design

- For screen widths ≤ **768px**, blocks are ~45% wide (two per row).
- For ≤**480px**, blocks are full width (one per row).

Output only the CSS code. Do not add explanations, comments, or other text.

Summary

In this chapter, we learned how to create a home page and its corresponding stylesheet. We also learned how to prompt AI to generate the necessary code. In the next chapter, we will learn about the continent landing page.

CHAPTER 10

Continent Page: North America

The home page allows navigation to five different continents, each with listed attractions. These continent pages, like the home page, are static and organized hierarchically for straightforward access to various locations and points of interest. This chapter will examine one continent in detail to demonstrate the code structure and website layout. The layout of the other continents is similar and will be briefly discussed at the end of the chapter. The continent we will explore is North America. Once you click on the North America block from the home page, the following screen is displayed.

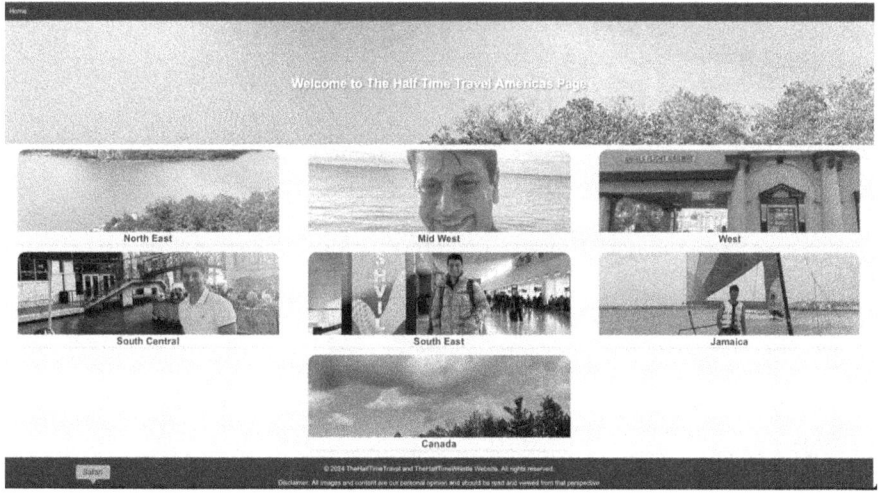

The continent page is exactly like the home page. The layout and functionality are the same (except for the introduction content). The only difference is that it always calls the region file with the area selected as input to the region file. In other words,

CHAPTER 10   CONTINENT PAGE: NORTH AMERICA

if Northeast is selected, the page will call the file region with "NorthEast" as the input. Based on this unique key, the region file would retrieve the relevant content from the MongoDB database, which we will explore in the next chapter.

Imports

All the necessary system and project-level imports are called in this section.

```
import React from 'react';
import { Helmet } from 'react-helmet-async';
import { Link, useNavigate } from 'react-router-dom';
import './HomePage.css';
import northeast from '../assets/northamerica.jpg';
import midwest from '../assets/midwest.jpg';
import west from '../assets/la.jpg';
import southcentral from '../assets/southcentral.jpg';
import jamaica from '../assets/jamaica.jpg';
import southeast from '../assets/southeast.jpg';
import canada from '../assets/canada.jpg';
const regions = [
  {
    name: 'North East',
    image: northeast,
    alt: 'Northeast USA Travel Destinations',
    path: '/northeast',
    regionState: 'NorthEast',
  },
  {
    name: 'Mid West',
    image: midwest,
    alt: 'Midwest USA Travel Destinations',
    path: '/midwest',
    regionState: 'MidWest',
  },
  {
```

```
    name: 'West',
    image: west,
    alt: 'West USA Travel Destinations',
    path: '/west',
    regionState: 'West',
  },
  {
    name: 'South Central',
    image: southcentral,
    alt: 'South Central USA Travel Destinations',
    path: '/southcentral',
    regionState: 'SouthCentral',
  },
  {
    name: 'South East',
    image: southeast,
    alt: 'South East USA Travel Destinations',
    path: '/southeast',
    regionState: 'SouthEast',
  },
  {
    name: 'Jamaica',
    image: jamaica,
    alt: 'Jamaica Travel Destinations',
    path: '/jamaica',
    regionState: 'Jamaica',
  },
  {
    name: 'Canada',
    image: canada,
    alt: 'Canada Travel Destinations',
    path: '/canada',
    regionState: 'Canada',
  },
];
```

The following are the key import statements called:

- **React**: Core library for building UIs.
- **Helmet**: React Helmet is used to manage changes to the document head (like title, meta tags). This is critical for SEO.
- **Link, useNavigate**: React Router v6+ hooks and components, critical for navigation to other pages:
    - **Link**: For in-app navigation links without full reload
    - **useNavigate**: A hook to programmatically navigate routes
- **HomePage.css**: Styles specific to this component. Note, since this page is exactly the same as the home page, we are leveraging the same CSS.
- **Image imports**: Various images for different North America regions imported as modules for display purposes.

Navigation Component

38% of users say that they will stop engaging with a web app if the navigation is overly confusing. It's important to have a simple navigation layout for this reason.

The code in this section defines the component and enables navigation to other pages based on user interaction with the page.

```
const NorthAmerica = () => {
  const navigate = useNavigate();

  const handleBlockClick = (destination, region) => {
    navigate(`/${destination.toLowerCase()}`, { state: { region:
    region } });
  };
```

Once the page component is defined, we define the navigation code:

- **useNavigate**: Hook to get the navigation function to move the user programmatically to other routes.

- **handleBlockClick**: A function that takes two parameters (destination, region). It calls navigate to a route based on the lowercased destination. It also passes the region as a route state, which can be accessed in the target route. In our case, the destination is always "region", and the region will be the block the user clicks on (e.g., "NorthEast").

Metadata Management

This section is for SEO (Search Engine Optimization) management.

```
<Helmet>
      <title>North America Travel Guide | The Half Time Travel</title>
      <meta name="description" content="Explore North America with The
      Half Time Travel. Discover the Northeast, Midwest, West, South
      Central regions,Jamaica, and Canada." />
      <meta property="og:title" content="North America Travel Guide | The
      Half Time Travel" />
      <meta property="og:description" content="Plan your North American
      adventure with The Half Time Travel. Explore diverse regions from
      the USA to Canada!" />
      <meta property="og:image" content={northeast} />
      <script type="application/ld+json">
        {JSON.stringify({
          "@context": "https://schema.org",
          "@type": "TravelBlog",
          "name": "The Half Time Travel - North America",
          "description": "Explore North America with The Half Time Travel",
          "url": "https://www.thehalftimewhistle.com/northamerica",
          "image": northeast
        })}
      </script>
</Helmet>
```

CHAPTER 10 CONTINENT PAGE: NORTH AMERICA

This piece of code manages the HTML <head> section for SEO so that search engines can easily find our web application. Key functions are

- Sets the document title
- Adds meta tags for description and Open Graph for better social media sharing
- Includes structured data (schema.org Travel Blog data) as JSON-LD for search engines

Header Section

This section defines the header of the page.

```
<header className="header">
     <nav className="nav-menu">
       <ul className="menu-level-1">
         <li><Link to="/">Home</Link></li>
       </ul>
     </nav>
     <div className="banner">
       <img src={northeast} alt="North America Travel Banner"
       className="banner-image" loading="eager" />
       <h1 className="banner-text">Welcome to The Half Time Travel
       Americas Page</h1>
     </div>
</header>
```

The header of the page has the following components:

- **Navigation**: Simple nav with a link to the home page ("/")
- **Banner**: Shows the banner image (northeast image) with an accessible alt tag and eager loading (this helps to load the page faster, even if the image is still loading)
- Heading welcome text on top of the banner

Main Content

This is the core part of the page where different areas within the North America page are drawn. Please note, tomorrow, if I visit a new country or an area, part of this code needs to be replicated to show the same, as the page is static.

```
<main className="main-content">
        <section className="content-blocks">
          {regions.map(({ name, image, alt, path, regionState }) => (
            <Link
              to={path}
              state={{ region: regionState }}
              className="block"
              key={name}
            >
              <article className="block-content">
                <img src={image} alt={alt} loading="eager" />
                <h2>{name}</h2>
              </article>
            </Link>
          ))}
        </section>
      </main>
```

The page has multiple div blocks or sections. Each section demonstrates the following:

- Section with clickable articles – each representing a travel region within that continent.

- Each <article> has an onClick handler calling handleBlockClick, passing

    - "Region" as a destination string (which is converted to lowercase and navigated to "/region").

    - A specific region name (like "NorthEast", "West", etc.) as route state. Based on this data parameter, content is retrieved from the database in the region component.

- Each block shows a representative image and a heading with the region name.
- The images use loading="eager" for performance optimization.
- All images and related data are organized in a single region array.
- Using a map over regions to dynamically render link components.
- Link includes the state with the region for navigation clarity.
- Keyboard and screen-reader accessible links instead of clickable <article>.
- SEO and structured metadata are maintained in Helmet.

Footer Section

This is the last part of the page, which is the disclaimer and privacy notice of the site.

```
<footer className="footer">
  <p>&copy; {new Date().getFullYear()} TheHalfTimeTravel and
  TheHalfTimeWhistle Website. All rights reserved.</p>
  <p>Disclaimer: All images and content are our personal opinion and should
  be read and viewed from that perspective</p>
</footer>
 </div>
```

This section contains the copyright and disclaimer about content ownership and opinion.

Complete Code

```
import React from 'react';
import React from 'react';
import { Helmet } from 'react-helmet-async';
import { Link, useNavigate } from 'react-router-dom';
import './HomePage.css';
```

```
// Import images
import northeast from '../assets/northamerica.jpg';
import midwest from '../assets/midwest.jpg';
import west from '../assets/la.jpg';
import southcentral from '../assets/southcentral.JPG';
import jamaica from '../assets/jamaica.jpg';
import southeast from '../assets/southeast.jpg';
import canada from '../assets/canada.jpg';

// Helper to convert string to kebab-case
const toKebabCase = (str) =>
  str &&
  str
    .match(/[A-Z]{2,}(?=[A-Z][a-z]+[0-9]*|\b)|[A-Z]?[a-z]+[0-9]*|[A-Z]|[0-9]+/g)
    .map(x => x.toLowerCase())
    .join('-');

const regions = [
  { name: 'North East', image: northeast, regionState: 'NorthEast' },
  { name: 'Mid West', image: midwest, regionState: 'MidWest' },
  { name: 'West', image: west, regionState: 'West' },
  { name: 'South Central', image: southcentral, regionState:
  'SouthCentral' },
  { name: 'South East', image: southeast, regionState: 'SouthEast' },
  { name: 'Jamaica', image: jamaica, regionState: 'Jamaica' },
  { name: 'Canada', image: canada, regionState: 'Canada' },
];

const NorthAmerica = () => {
  const navigate = useNavigate();

  const handleBlockClick = (destination, region) => {
    const slug = toKebabCase(destination);
    navigate(`/region/${slug}`, { state: { region } });
  };

  return (
```

CHAPTER 10   CONTINENT PAGE: NORTH AMERICA

```jsx
<>
  <Helmet>
    <title>North America Travel Guide | The Half Time Travel</title>
    <meta
      name="description"
      content="Explore North America with The Half Time Travel.
        Discover the Northeast, Midwest, West, South Central regions,
        Jamaica, and Canada."
    />
    <meta
      property="og:title"
      content="North America Travel Guide | The Half Time Travel"
    />
    <meta
      property="og:description"
      content="Plan your North American adventure with The Half Time
        Travel. Explore diverse regions from the USA to Canada!"
    />
    <meta property="og:image" content={northeast} />
    <script type="application/ld+json">
      {JSON.stringify({
        "@context": "https://schema.org",
        "@type": "TravelBlog",
        name: "The Half Time Travel - North America",
        description: "Explore North America with The Half Time Travel",
        url: "https://www.thehalftimewhistle.com/northamerica",
        image: northeast,
      })}
    </script>
  </Helmet>

  <div className="home-page">
    <header className="header">
      <nav className="nav-menu">
        <ul className="menu-level-1">
          <li>
```

```jsx
          <Link to="/">Home</Link>
        </li>
      </ul>
    </nav>
    <div className="banner">
      <img
        src={northeast}
        alt="North America Travel Banner"
        className="banner-image"
        loading="eager"
      />
      <h1 className="banner-text">Welcome to The Half Time Travel
      Americas Page</h1>
    </div>
  </header>

  <main className="main-content">
    <section className="content-blocks">
      {regions.map((({ name, image, regionState }) => (
        // Option 1: clickable div with onClick (kept for
        demonstration, not recommended for accessibility)
        /*
        <article
          key={name}
          className="block"
          tabIndex={0}
          role="button"
          onClick={() => handleBlockClick(name, regionState)}
          onKeyDown={(e) => {
            if (e.key === 'Enter' || e.key === ' ') {
              e.preventDefault();
              handleBlockClick(name, regionState);
            }
          }}
        >
          <div className="block-content">
```

```
              <img src={image} alt={`${name} Travel Destinations`}
              loading="eager" />
              <h2>{name}</h2>
            </div>
          </article>
          */

          // Option 2 (Recommended): use Link with URL and route state
          <Link
            key={name}
            to={`/region/${toKebabCase(name)}`}
            state={{ region: regionState }}
            className="block"
          >
            <article className="block-content">
              <img src={image} alt={`${name} Travel Destinations`}
              loading="eager" />
              <h2>{name}</h2>
            </article>
          </Link>
        ))}
      </section>
    </main>

<footer className="footer">
  <p>&copy; {new Date().getFullYear()} TheHalfTimeTravel and
  TheHalfTimeWhistle Website. All rights reserved.</p>
  <p>Disclaimer: All images and content are our personal opinion and should
  be read and viewed from that perspective</p>
</footer>      </div>
    </>
  );
};

export default NorthAmerica;
```

CHAPTER 10   CONTINENT PAGE: NORTH AMERICA

AI Prompt

Here is a detailed AI prompt you can use to generate the provided React code:

AI Prompt

Create a React functional component named `NorthAmerica` for a travel website called "The Half Time Travel". The component should display clickable travel regions in North America with images and allow navigation to a region-specific page when each region is clicked. Implement the following requirements:

- Imports:
  - Import React.
  - Import `Helmet` from `react-helmet` to manage SEO metadata.
  - Import `Link` and `useNavigate` from `react-router-dom` for navigation.
  - Import a CSS file named `HomePage.css` for styling.
  - Import the following images from local assets:
  - northeast from '../assets/northamerica.jpg'
  - midwest from '../assets/midwest.jpg'
  - west from '../assets/la.jpg'
  - southcentral from '../assets/southcentral.JPG'
  - jamaica from '../assets/jamaica.jpg'
  - southeast from '../assets/southeast.jpg'
  - canada from '../assets/canada.jpg'

- Component Functionality:
  - Use semantic, accessible <Link> components with their to prop set to /region/:slug and state prop passing the region for direct declarative navigation.
  - Using <Link> components instead of clickable elements to improve keyboard accessibility, enhancing screen reader support, and benefiting SEO.

CHAPTER 10   CONTINENT PAGE: NORTH AMERICA

- JSX Structure:
  - Use `<Helmet>` to set document metadata:
  - Title: "North America Travel Guide | The Half Time Travel"
  - Meta description describing exploration of North America regions including Northeast, Midwest, West, South Central, Jamaica, and Canada.
  - Open Graph title and description reflecting the same.
  - Open Graph image using the northeast image.
  - Include JSON-LD structured data (schema.org TravelBlog) with name, description, URL (https://www.thehalftimewhistle.com/northamerica), and image set to the northeast image.
  - Render a root `<div>` with class `home-page` containing:
  - Header:
  - A navigation menu linking back to the homepage ("/").
  - A banner image using the northeast image with alt text `North America Travel Banner`, styled with class `banner-image`, and eager loading enabled.
  - A welcoming heading text: `Welcome to The Half Time Travel Americas Page`.
  - Main Content:
  - A `<section>` with class `content-blocks` containing seven clickable `<article>` blocks.
  - Each block:
  - Has an onClick handler that calls handleBlockClick('Region', regionName), where regionName is one of:
  - "NorthEast"
  - "MidWest"
  - "West"

- "SouthCentral"
- "SouthEast"
- "Jamaica"
- "Canada"
- Displays an image representing that region with appropriate alt text (e.g., `"Northeast USA Travel Destinations"`) and eager loading.
- Contains an `<h2>` heading with the region name displayed in natural language (e.g., `"North East"` for `"NorthEast"`).
- Footer:
- Contains copyright:
- `"Year to be automatically created based on the current year` TheHalfTimeTravel and TheHalfTimeWhistle Website. All rights reserved."
- A disclaimer paragraph: "Disclaimer: All images and content are our personal opinion and should be read and viewed from that perspective".
- Additional Requirements:
  - Use React fragments ( ) around the component output.
  - Export the component as the default export of the module.

End Prompt

Please note the amount of detail provided to the AI LLM model to ensure an accurate code is generated.

CHAPTER 10   CONTINENT PAGE: NORTH AMERICA

Summary

In this chapter, we continued building our website journey and created the continent page, which is displayed when the user selects a continent. Please note that this is a static page, and in this chapter, we learned to create one of the five continents. To complete the web application, we need to create the reminder of pages in a similar way. Next, we will learn to create the region page, which displays regions traveled to in a particular area in a specific continent.

CHAPTER 11

Region Page

So far, we have created the home page, learned the continent navigation page, and delved into the stylesheet that renders the page optimally and aesthetically across devices. We have also learned some of the core concepts of React, like the inclusion of Helmet for SEO and useNavigate to help route between pages. Each chapter also summarized the AI prompt we could use to create the code using an LLM model.

The pages so far were static, but in this chapter, we will learn to create a React component that is dynamic in nature and retrieves information from a database (MongoDB) for display based on user interaction with the web application. We will also learn how the same code can be used to repurpose any number of contents without modifying the code.

The region React component takes in one parameter (the region) and displays an image and a small teaser blurb of the content in a block form. The block is clickable, and upon clicking, it invokes another page to display the details of the selected travel interest area – this part we would learn in the next chapter.

Continuing with our example, let us assume the user selects North America as the continent and then the NorthEast as the region. The region page will then display the following:

CHAPTER 11   REGION PAGE

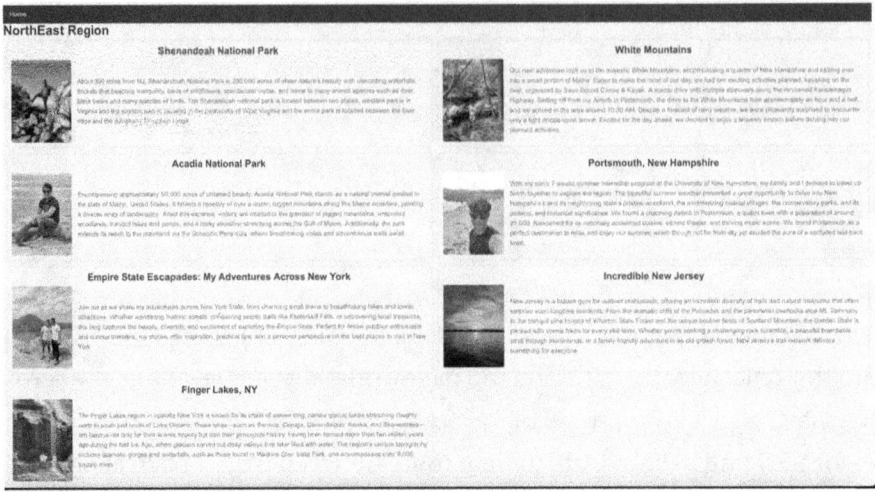

Let us now learn how this page is built.

Key Implementation Concepts

- **Dynamic Region**: The viewed region is based on route state or defaults to "NorthEast".

- **Data Fetching**: Asynchronous; handles loading and error scenarios robustly.

- **Dynamic Image Imports**: Uses dynamic JS import() for per-place images (for code-splitting and lazy loading).

- **SEO**: Uses Helmet to add region-specific SEO metadata.

- **Navigation**: Integrates smoothly with React Router for single-page app navigation.

Example User Flow

- User navigates to this page after selecting a region from the Continent page.

- Component fetches places for the selected region.

- Renders a list of places (with title, image name, and description).
- User clicks a block of content and navigates to a detailed page for that place (to be discussed in the next chapter).
- SEO/OG tags reflect the region for sharing/social media.

Imports

All required system and user-defined packages and components are imported for the region component to function.

```
import React, { useState, useEffect, useRef } from 'react';
import { Helmet } from 'react-helmet';
import { Link, useNavigate, useLocation } from 'react-router-dom';
import DOMPurify from 'dompurify';
import './HomePage.css';
import './ItemsStyle.css';
```

The following are the key imports:

- **React, useState, useEffect, useRef**: Core React library and two hooks for managing state and side effects.
- **Helmet:** Allows manipulation of the document head for SEO enablement and social sharing tags.
- **Link, useNavigate, useLocation:** From react-router-dom for client-side routing and navigation.
- **HomePage.css, ItemsStyle.css:** CSS files for styling. We have discussed HomePage.css. In this chapter, we will go into details on ItemsStyle.css.

Component Definition: Region

The core React component definition of the page, where content gets displayed and back-end MongoDB calls are made.

CHAPTER 11 REGION PAGE

```
// Whitelisted images map with intrinsic dimensions
const imageWhitelist = {
  'place1.jpg': { url: 'https://cdn.statically.io/gh/shantpinku/
  halftimewhistle-cdn/master/place1.jpg', width: 400, height: 300 },
  'place2.jpg': { url: 'https://cdn.statically.io/gh/shantpinku/
  halftimewhistle-cdn/master/place2.jpg', width: 320, height: 240 },
  // Add all allowed images here with their dimensions
};

const getRegionFromUrl = (pathname) => {
  // Assuming URL structure: /region/:regionName
  const match = pathname.match(/\/region\/([^/]+)/);
  return match ? match[1] : 'NorthEast';
};

const Region = () => {
  const navigate = useNavigate();
  const location = useLocation();
  const [places, setPlaces] = useState([]);
  const [isLoading, setIsLoading] = useState(true);
  const [error, setError] = useState(null);
  const abortControllerRef = useRef(null);

  // Calculate region from URL for deep linking
  const region = getRegionFromUrl(location.pathname);
```

Region Calculation from URL

- The function parses the region directly from location.pathname for deep linking and page reload resiliency.

Dynamic Import Replaced by Whitelisted Map

- The hard-coded whitelist mapping image file names to URLs and intrinsic dimensions, all served via the Statically CDN (GitHub pages), avoiding risky dynamic import

The following are Router Hooks and State defined in the region component. Please note that there is more code to the component, which we will discuss in the next sections.

- **navigate**: Lets us change routes programmatically.
- **location**: Gives access to the current route's location object (including state).
- **region**: Extracted from location.state?.region; defaults to "NorthEast" if not provided.
- **places**: State array holding data about places in the region.
- **isLoading**: Indicates whether data is still loading.
- **error**: Holds errors encountered when fetching places.

Fetching Data with useEffect

This function helps in getting data from our back-end database.

```
useEffect(() => {
    // Memory leak/race condition prevention
    abortControllerRef.current?.abort();
    const abortController = new AbortController();
    abortControllerRef.current = abortController;
    setIsLoading(true);
    setError(null);
```

Memory Leaks, Race Conditions, Stale UI

- AbortController via useRef will safely abort old fetches on component unmount or region change. This mitigates memory leaks and race conditions.

fetchPlaces Function

This function will get the data from MongoDB based on the region parameter.

```
const fetchPlaces = async () => {
    try {
        const response = await fetch(
```

```
      `/api/places/${encodeURIComponent(region.toLowerCase())}`,
      { signal: abortController.signal }
    );
    if (!response.ok) {
      throw new Error(`HTTP error! status: ${response.status}`);
    }
    const data = await response.json();
    if (!Array.isArray(data.data)) {
      throw new Error('Data is not an array');
    }
    setPlaces(data.data);
  } catch (e) {
    if (e.name !== 'AbortError') {
      console.error('Fetch error:', e);
      setError(`Failed to fetch places for ${region}. Error:
      ${e.message}`);
    }
  } finally {
    setIsLoading(false);
  }
};

fetchPlaces();

// Cleanup function to prevent memory leaks
return () => {
  abortController.abort();
};
}, [region, location.pathname]);
```

This function performs the following function:

- Fetches data for the current region from /api/places/{region}
- Handles errors:
    - If the HTTP request fails, sets an error message
    - If the returned data isn't an array, also errors out

CHAPTER 11　REGION PAGE

- On success: Stores the array in places and clears any previous error

- On completion: Sets isLoading to false

PlaceComponent

The region component displays only teaser content of the place visited. Once a place of interest is selected, this navigation function is triggered, which navigates to another React component to fetch the relevant details of the page.

This function displays the places visited for a particular region. The function returns the title, image name, and description of the places.

```
const PlaceComponent = ({ place }) => {
    let imageData = place.image ? imageWhitelist[place.image] : null;

    // Responsive images for layout shift reduction
    const getImageSrcSet = (imgKey) => {
      if (!imgKey) return '';
      // Example: create srcset for different resolutions (using statically
      CDN resize)
      return `
        https://cdn.statically.io/img/cdn.statically.io/gh/shantpinku/
        halftimewhistle-cdn/master/${imgKey}?w=240 240w,
        https://cdn.statically.io/img/cdn.statically.io/gh/shantpinku/
        halftimewhistle-cdn/master/${imgKey}?w=400 400w
      `;
    };
```

Navigates to /ContentDisplayOne, passing

- The region

- The place's title and its _id via router state

Layout Shift and Responsive Images

- Width and height of images from a whitelisted map are added for intrinsic dimensions.

183

- Responsive srcSet images from the CDN are added for layout stability and smaller images on smaller screens.

A nested component that

- Displays title, image, and description for a place.
- Tries to load an image for the place using a dynamic import. Please note that the database only stores the name of the image. The actual image is stored in the web server.
- On success: Sets the image URL in the state for display.
- On error: Displays a fallback message.

Rendering Content

This code renders the content and makes it clickable.

```
return (
    <article className="item">
      <Link
        className="item-link"
        to="/ContentDisplayOne"
        state={{
          region,
          title: place.title,
          id: place._id
        }}
      >
        <h2>{DOMPurify.sanitize(place.title) || 'No Title'}</h2>
        <div className="item-content">
          {imageData ? (
            <img
              src={imageData.url}
              srcSet={getImageSrcSet(place.image)}
              alt={DOMPurify.sanitize(place.title) || 'No Title'}
              width={imageData.width}
```

```
            height={imageData.height}
            loading="lazy"
            style={{ objectFit: 'cover', maxWidth: '100%', height:
            'auto' }}
          />
        ) : (
          <div>Image not available</div>
        )}
        <p
          dangerouslySetInnerHTML={{
            __html: DOMPurify.sanitize(place.description || 'No
            Description'),
          }}
        />
      </div>
    </Link>
  </article>
);
};

if (isLoading) return <div>Loading...</div>;
if (error) return <div>{error}</div>;
```

This piece of content helps render the content using an HTML5 code snippet. The code is iterated for the total number of places returned from the database.

- The navigation is using semantic <Link> wrapping the content, which improves accessibility and reliability.

- The class name is defined in the CSS, which helps style the content block. We will learn this in this chapter in detail.

- The entire article is clickable and selects the place (via handlePlaceSelect).

- The block renders the title, image, and description fetched from the database.

- The following two are the State-Dependent Returns:
  - **Loading**: If isLoading is true, shows "Loading..."
  - **Error**: If there's an error, displays it

Content Render Structure

```
return (
  <>
    <Helmet>
      <title>{`${region} Travel Guide | The Half Time Travel`}</title>
      <meta name="description" content={`Explore ${region} with The Half Time Travel. Discover amazing destinations and travel tips.`} />
      <meta property="og:title" content={`${region} Travel Guide | The Half Time Travel`} />
      <meta property="og:description" content={`Plan your ${region} adventure with The Half Time Travel. Explore top destinations and hidden gems!`} />
      <script type="application/ld+json">
        {JSON.stringify({
          "@context": "https://schema.org",
          "@type": "TravelBlog",
          "name": `The Half Time Travel - ${region}`,
          "description": `Explore ${region} with The Half Time Travel`,
          "url": `https://www.thehalftimewhistle.com/${region.toLowerCase()}`
        })}
      </script>
    </Helmet>
    <div className="home-page">
      <header className="header">
        <nav className="nav-menu">
          <ul className="menu-level-1">
            <li><Link to="/">Home</Link></li>
```

```
          </ul>
        </nav>
      </header>
      <main>
        <h1>{region} Region</h1>
        <section className="items-container">
          {places.length > 0 ? (
            places.map((place) => (
              <PlaceComponent
                key={place._id}
                place={place}
              />
            ))
          ) : (
            <p>No places found for {region}</p>
          )}
        </section>
      </main>
      <footer className="footer">
        <p>&copy; 2024 TheHalfTimeTravel and TheHalfTimeWhistle Website.
        All rights reserved.</p>
        <p>Disclaimer: All images and content are our personal opinion
        and should be read and viewed from that perspective</p>
      </footer>
    </div>
  </>
  );
};
export default Region;
```

Layout Shift and Responsive Images

- Added width and height to images from a whitelisted map for intrinsic dimensions

- Provided responsive srcSet images from the CDN for layout stability and smaller images on smaller screens

CHAPTER 11 REGION PAGE

XSS Protection

- Integrated DOMPurify for sanitizing both the title and description, covering any user-generated or dynamic HTML/descriptions

Dynamic Import Replaced by Whitelisted Map

- Used a hard-coded whitelist mapping image file names to URLs and intrinsic dimensions, all served via the Statically CDN, avoiding risky dynamic import

Helmet

- Sets the page <title>, meta description, Open Graph tags, and some structured data (JSON-LD travel blog data)

Page Layout

- Header: Contains a navigation menu ("Home")
- **Main Content**
    - Displays the region name.
    - A section listing all places using PlaceComponent. If none, displays "No places found".
    - **Footer**: Copyright and disclaimer.

Complete Code

```
import React, { useState, useEffect, useRef } from 'react';
import { Helmet } from 'react-helmet';
import { Link, useNavigate, useLocation } from 'react-router-dom';
import DOMPurify from 'dompurify';
import './HomePage.css';
import './ItemsStyle.css';

// Whitelisted images map with intrinsic dimensions
const imageWhitelist = {
  'place1.jpg': { url: 'https://cdn.statically.io/gh/shantpinku/
  halftimewhistle-cdn/master/place1.jpg', width: 400, height: 300 },
```

```
  'place2.jpg': { url: 'https://cdn.statically.io/gh/shantpinku/
  halftimewhistle-cdn/master/place2.jpg', width: 320, height: 240 },
  // Add all allowed images here with their dimensions
};

const getRegionFromUrl = (pathname) => {
  // Assuming URL structure: /region/:regionName
  const match = pathname.match(/\/region\/([^/]+)/);
  return match ? match[1] : 'NorthEast';
};

const Region = () => {
  const navigate = useNavigate();
  const location = useLocation();
  const [places, setPlaces] = useState();
  const [isLoading, setIsLoading] = useState(true);
  const [error, setError] = useState(null);
  const abortControllerRef = useRef(null);

  // Calculate region from URL for deep linking
  const region = getRegionFromUrl(location.pathname);

  useEffect(() => {
    // Memory leak/race condition prevention
    abortControllerRef.current?.abort();
    const abortController = new AbortController();
    abortControllerRef.current = abortController;
    setIsLoading(true);
    setError(null);

    const fetchPlaces = async () => {
      try {
        const response = await fetch(
          `/api/places/${encodeURIComponent(region.toLowerCase())}`,
          { signal: abortController.signal }
        );
        if (!response.ok) {
          throw new Error(`HTTP error! status: ${response.status}`);
```

```
        }
        const data = await response.json();
        if (!Array.isArray(data.data)) {
          throw new Error('Data is not an array');
        }
        setPlaces(data.data);
      } catch (e) {
        if (e.name !== 'AbortError') {
          console.error('Fetch error:', e);
          setError(`Failed to fetch places for ${region}. Error: ${e.
          message}`);
        }
      } finally {
        setIsLoading(false);
      }
    };

    fetchPlaces();

    // Cleanup function to prevent memory leaks
    return () => {
      abortController.abort();
    };
  }, [region, location.pathname]);
  const PlaceComponent = ({ place }) => {
    let imageData = place.image ? imageWhitelist[place.image] : null;

    // Responsive images for layout shift reduction
    const getImageSrcSet = (imgKey) => {
      if (!imgKey) return '';
      // Example: create srcset for different resolutions (using statically
      CDN resize)
      return `
        https://cdn.statically.io/img/cdn.statically.io/gh/shantpinku/
        halftimewhistle-cdn/master/${imgKey}?w=240 240w,
```

```
      https://cdn.statically.io/img/cdn.statically.io/gh/shantpinku/
      halftimewhistle-cdn/master/${imgKey}?w=400 400w
  `;
};

return (
  <article className="item">
    <Link
      className="item-link"
      to="/ContentDisplayOne"
      state={{
        region,
        title: place.title,
        id: place._id
      }}
    >
      <h2>{DOMPurify.sanitize(place.title) || 'No Title'}</h2>
      <div className="item-content">
        {imageData ? (
          <img
            src={imageData.url}
            srcSet={getImageSrcSet(place.image)}
            alt={DOMPurify.sanitize(place.title) || 'No Title'}
            width={imageData.width}
            height={imageData.height}
            loading="lazy"
            style={{ objectFit: 'cover', maxWidth: '100%', height:
            'auto' }}
          />
        ) : (
          <div>Image not available</div>
        )}
        <p
          dangerouslySetInnerHTML={{
            __html: DOMPurify.sanitize(place.description || 'No
            Description'),
```

```
            }}
          />
        </div>
      </Link>
    </article>
  );
};

if (isLoading) return <div>Loading...</div>;
if (error) return <div>{error}</div>;

return (
  <>
    <Helmet>
      <title>{`${region} Travel Guide | The Half Time Travel`}</title>
      <meta name="description" content={`Explore ${region} with The Half
      Time Travel. Discover amazing destinations and travel tips.`} />
      <meta property="og:title" content={`${region} Travel Guide | The
      Half Time Travel`} />
      <meta property="og:description" content={`Plan your ${region}
      adventure with The Half Time Travel. Explore top destinations and
      hidden gems!`} />
      <script type="application/ld+json">
        {JSON.stringify({
          "@context": "https://schema.org",
          "@type": "TravelBlog",
          "name": `The Half Time Travel - ${region}`,
          "description": `Explore ${region} with The Half Time Travel`,
          "url": `https://www.thehalftimewhistle.com/${region.
          toLowerCase()}`
        })}
      </script>
    </Helmet>
    <div className="home-page">
      <header className="header">
        <nav className="nav-menu">
          <ul className="menu-level-1">
```

```
            <li><Link to="/">Home</Link></li>
          </ul>
        </nav>
      </header>
      <main>
        <h1>{region} Region</h1>
        <section className="items-container">
          {places.length > 0 ? (
            places.map((place) => (
              <PlaceComponent
                key={place._id}
                place={place}
              />
            ))
          ) : (
            <p>No places found for {region}</p>
          )}
        </section>
      </main>
      <footer className="footer">
        <p>&copy; 2024 TheHalfTimeTravel and TheHalfTimeWhistle Website.
        All rights reserved.</p>
        <p>Disclaimer: All images and content are our personal opinion
        and should be read and viewed from that perspective</p>
      </footer>
    </div>
  </>
  );
};

export default Region;
```

CHAPTER 11   REGION PAGE

AI Prompt

Prompt

Write a React functional component named Region for a travel guide app with these features:

- Use React hooks — useState, useEffect, and useRef — to manage state, handle side effects, and store an abort controller reference for fetch cancellation.

- Use React Router's useNavigate and useLocation hooks to navigate programmatically and read the current URL.

- Determine the region dynamically from the URL pathname (assumed format /region/:regionName) with a fallback default region.

Maintain state for:

- places (array of destination objects),

- isLoading (boolean for fetch status),

- error (string or null for fetch errors).

In useEffect, fetch place data from /api/places/${region} endpoint:

- Cancel previous fetch on region change or component unmount using AbortController,

- Handle HTTP errors and data validation,

- Update loading and error states accordingly.

- Use a whitelist object mapping approved image filenames to trusted CDN URLs plus intrinsic width and height for optimized image rendering.

Create a PlaceComponent child that:

- Accepts a place prop with title, description, _id, and image,

- Sanitizes dynamic HTML/text fields using DOMPurify,

- Loads images from the whitelist with responsive srcSet attributes for better layout stability,

- Wraps content in React Router's <Link> for accessible client-side navigation, passing region, title, and id in navigation state.

Use react-helmet to set document <title>, meta description, OpenGraph tags, and embed structured data (JSON-LD) dynamically based on region.

Render:

- A header with navigation link to Home,
- Main content with a list of places using PlaceComponent,
- Loading and error UI as appropriate,
- A footer with copyright and disclaimer.

Import necessary libraries: React, Helmet, React Router hooks, DOMPurify, and CSS stylesheets for layout and items styling.

Export the Region component as default.

Include inline comments explaining key implementation details like abort controller usage, URL region parsing, image whitelisting, XSS protection via sanitization, and SEO metadata.

Stylesheet for Region Component

In this section, we will learn about the stylesheet used to render the design for the region.js page. Please note that region.js also uses HomePage.css, which we learned before and ItemStyle.css only contains incremental stylesheet designs. The ITemStyle.css has the following core design principles:

- **Layout**: Blocks are arranged side by side in a responsive grid, stacking on small screens.
- **Blocks**: Each block is stylish - rounded corners, shadows, hover effect, and clickable.
- **Content**: Each block has a centered title, side-by-side (or stacked on mobile) image and text.
- **Responsiveness**: Looks clean and readable on both desktop and mobile devices.

CHAPTER 11   REGION PAGE

- **User Experience**: Visual feedback on hovering cards, images sized consistently, and mobile-friendly adjustments.

It's important for a web application to look good on both desktop and mobile devices. This is because 90% of users use multiple screens when completing tasks and alternate once they trust your website. It's important to be consistent with runtimes for this reason so you don't lose your users.

The Container

```
.items-container {
  display: flex;
  flex-wrap: wrap;
  justify-content: space-between;
  max-width: 100%;
  margin: 0 auto;
  padding: 10px;
}
```

- **display: flex;:** Makes the container a flexbox for easy horizontal layout of children
- **flex-wrap: wrap;** Allows flex items to wrap to the next line if they overflow the width
- **justify-content: space-between;:** Distributes child items with space between, pushing the first and last items to the edges
- **max-width: 100%;:** Makes sure the container doesn't exceed the window width
- **margin: 0 auto;:** Centers the container horizontally (has effect when a width is set)
- **padding: 10px;:** Adds space inside the container around its contents

.item

```
.item {
  width: calc(50% - 10px);
  margin-bottom: 20px;
  padding: 10px;
  box-shadow: 0 0 10px rgba(0, 0, 0, 0.1);
  border-radius: 8px;
  box-sizing: border-box;
  transition: all 0.3s ease; /* Add smooth transition for hover effects */
  cursor: pointer; /* Change cursor to pointer on hover */
}
```

- **width: calc (50% - 10px);:** Makes each item take half the container's width, accounting for spacing
- **margin-bottom: 20px;:** Adds space below each item
- **padding: 10px;:** Adds inner spacing inside the card
- **box-shadow:** Gives a subtle shadow around each card for depth
- **border-radius: 8px;:** Rounds the corners
- **box-sizing: border-box;:** Includes padding and border in the width calculation for consistency
- **transition: all 0.3s ease;:** Animates changes (like hover effects) smoothly
- **cursor: pointer;:** Shows a pointer cursor when hovering, indicating the card is clickable

.item:hover

```
.item:hover {
  transform: translateY(-5px); /* Slight lift effect on hover */
  box-shadow: 0 5px 15px rgba(0, 0, 0, 0.2); /* Stronger shadow on hover */
}
```

- **transform: translateY(-5px);:** Lifts the item slightly when hovered over
- **box-shadow:** Increases the shadow for a "floating" effect on hover

.item h2

```
.item h2 {
  margin-bottom: 10px;
  font-size: 1.5em;
  text-align: center;
}
```

- **margin-bottom: 10px;:** Separates the title from the rest of the card
- **font-size: 1.5em;:** Makes the title larger
- **text-align: center;:** Centers the heading text

.item-content

```
.item-content {
  display: flex;
  align-items: center;
}
```

- **display: flex;:** Lays out content (image and description) in a row
- **align-items: center;:** Vertically aligns the children in the center

.item img

```
.item img {
  width: 150px;
  height: auto;
  border-radius: 4px;
```

```
  margin-right: 15px;
}
```

- **width: 150px;:** Sets a fixed image width
- **height: auto;:** Keeps image aspect ratio
- **border-radius: 4px;:** Slightly rounds corners
- **margin-right: 15px;:** Spaces the image from the description

.item p

```
.item p {
  flex: 1;
  margin: 0;
  color: #666;
}
```

- **flex: 1;:** Expands the paragraph to fill the remaining space
- **margin: 0;:** Removes default space above/below the text
- **color: #666;:** Sets text color to a subtle gray

Responsive Design (Media Query for ≤768px)

```
@media (max-width: 768px) {
  .item {
    width: 100%;
  }
  .item-content {
    flex-direction: column;
  }
  .item img {
    margin-right: 0;
    margin-bottom: 10px;
```

- **.item { width: 100%; }:** Each card spans the full width, stacking vertically.

- **.item-content { flex-direction: column; }:** Image and description stack vertically instead of side-by-side.

- **.item img { margin-right: 0; margin-bottom: 10px; }:** Removes right margin and adds space beneath the image for better mobile presentation.

body Style

```
body {
  padding: 0 10px;
}
```

Adds horizontal padding so the entire page content doesn't touch the browser edge.

Complete Code

```
.items-container {
  display: flex;
  flex-wrap: wrap;
  justify-content: space-between;
  max-width: 100%;
  margin: 0 auto;
  padding: 10px;
}
.item {
  width: calc(50% - 10px);
  margin-bottom: 20px;
  padding: 10px;
```

```css
  box-shadow: 0 0 10px rgba(0, 0, 0, 0.1);
  border-radius: 8px;
  box-sizing: border-box;
  transition: all 0.3s ease; /* Add smooth transition for hover effects */
  cursor: pointer; /* Change cursor to pointer on hover */
}

.item:hover {
  transform: translateY(-5px); /* Slight lift effect on hover */
  box-shadow: 0 5px 15px rgba(0, 0, 0, 0.2); /* Stronger shadow on hover */
}

.item h2 {
  margin-bottom: 10px;
  font-size: 1.5em;
  text-align: center;
}

.item-content {
  display: flex;
  align-items: center;
}

.item img {
  width: 150px;
  height: auto;
  border-radius: 4px;
  margin-right: 15px;
}

.item p {
  flex: 1;
  margin: 0;
  color: #666;
}

@media (max-width: 768px) {
  .item {
```

```
    width: 100%;
  }
  .item-content {
    flex-direction: column;
  }
  .item img {
    margin-right: 0;
    margin-bottom: 10px;
  }
}
body {
  padding: 0 10px;
}
```

AI Prompt

Write a CSS stylesheet for a responsive card grid suitable for displaying a list of items (such as travel destinations). Style the following classes and elements:

.items-container

- Use Flexbox to layout its children in a row, allowing wrapping across lines as needed.
- Space the items evenly with space between.
- The container should not exceed the window width, and have some padding around it.

.item

- Each item should be displayed as a card, occupying roughly half the container's width, with some margin at the bottom.

- Add padding inside the card, rounded corners, and a subtle box shadow for depth.
- Ensure the box-sizing is border-box.
- Add a smooth transition effect for hover.
- Change the cursor to pointer on hover.

Hover state for .item

- On hover, lift the card slightly using translateY and make the shadow more prominent.

Titles inside .item (<h2>)

- Space the title from the rest of the content below.
- Make the title large and center-align the text.

.item-content

- Use Flexbox to arrange the image and description in a row, vertically centered.

Image inside .item

- Set a fixed width for images, keeping the aspect ratio.
- Slightly round the corners.
- Space the image from the text on the right.

Paragraph inside .item

- Allow the description to fill the available space.
- Remove default margins, and set text to a muted gray.

Responsive adjustments (for screens ≤ 768px):

- Stack the cards vertically (full width).
- Arrange the content inside .item-content in a column.
- Remove the right margin from images and add space beneath them.

body

- Apply horizontal padding so content doesn't touch screen edges.

Please include comments for clarity where needed. The resulting CSS should look modern, readable, responsive, and interactive for a clean card layout.

Summary

In this chapter, we learned how to fetch data from the back end, handle JSON objects for data retrieval, and content rendition based on modern design and stylesheet. In the next chapter, we will learn about creating our final React component to display the selected place details.

CHAPTER 12

Detail Travel Page

This is the final chapter of our travel web application development. In this chapter, we will learn the code that renders content, image carousel, detailed travel itineraries, and images. The page has many sections as defined below:

- A header section with a link to the menu and to navigate back to the region page. The header also has an image representation of the selected place.

- A clickable image carousel that lists the places the user visited in the current itinerary.

- A brief description of the place with the date of visit.

- A section on About the place with images displayed in a 4×4 matrix. Each image, when clicked, enlarges.

- A repeat of the section with other content display like experience, address, interesting facts, and other details.

The following screen shows how the page would look after development:

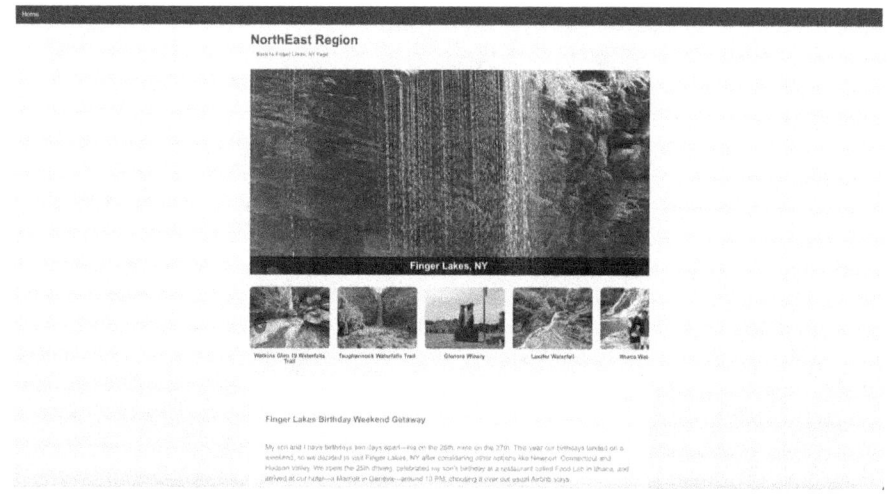

© Shantanu Baruah 2025
S. Baruah, *Generative AI for Full-Stack Development*, https://doi.org/10.1007/979-8-8688-2074-8_4

CHAPTER 12   DETAIL TRAVEL PAGE

Finger Lakes Birthday Weekend Getaway

My son and I have birthdays two days apart—his on the 25th, mine on the 27th. This year our birthdays landed on a weekend, so we decided to visit Finger Lakes, NY after considering other options like Newport, Connecticut and Hudson Valley. We spent the 25th driving, celebrated my son's birthday at a restaurant called Food Lab in Ithaca, and arrived at our hotel—a Marriott in Geneva—around 10 PM, checking it over our usual Airbnb stays.

Our exploration of the area was a combination of hiking, sightseeing, and soaking in the raw beauty of upstate New York.

Travel Date

25-Jul-25 to 25-Jul-25

About The Place

Finger Lakes Region – Overview & Highlights

The Finger Lakes region in upstate New York is known for its chain of eleven long, narrow glacial lakes stretching roughly north to south just south of Lake Ontario. These lakes—such as Seneca, Cayuga, Canandaigua, Keuka, and Skaneateles—are famous not only for their scenic beauty but also their geological history, having been formed more than two million years ago during the last Ice Age, when glaciers carved out deep valleys that later filled with water. The region's unique topography includes dramatic gorges and waterfalls, such as those found in Watkins Glen State Park, and encompasses over 9,000 square miles.

The Finger Lakes area is New York's premier wine-producing region, hosting over 400 wineries and vineyards that benefit from the lakes' moderating climate—this "lake effect" protects grapevines from extreme temperatures and supports the production of some of the finest Rieslings in North America. Beyond wine, the area offers a wealth of recreational activities, from kayaking and fishing to swimming and sailing, and is rich in American history, notably playing significant roles in the women's rights movement and the Underground Railroad. The combination of history, outdoor adventure, gorgeous landscapes, and robust agritourism makes the Finger Lakes region a top choice for us to explore this summer.

About The Place

Finger Lakes Region – Overview & Highlights

The Finger Lakes region in upstate New York is known for its chain of eleven long, narrow glacial lakes stretching roughly north to south just south of Lake Ontario. These lakes—such as Seneca, Cayuga, Canandaigua, Keuka, and Skaneateles—are famous not only for their scenic beauty but also their geological history, having been formed more than two million years ago during the last Ice Age, when glaciers carved out deep valleys that later filled with water. The region's unique topography includes dramatic gorges and waterfalls, such as those found in Watkins Glen State Park, and encompasses over 9,000 square miles.

The Finger Lakes area is New York's premier wine-producing region, hosting over 400 wineries and vineyards that benefit from the lakes' moderating climate—this "lake effect" protects grapevines from extreme temperatures and supports the production of some of the finest Rieslings in North America. Beyond wine, the area offers a wealth of recreational activities, from kayaking and fishing to swimming and sailing, and is rich in American history, notably playing significant roles in the women's rights movement and the Underground Railroad. The combination of history, outdoor adventure, gorgeous landscapes, and robust agritourism makes the Finger Lakes region a top choice for us to explore this summer.

What to Bring

Hiking Essentials & Safety Tips

- The walk has many boulders and steep climbs with slippery surfaces. Please plan to bring good hiking shoes.

206

CHAPTER 12 DETAIL TRAVEL PAGE

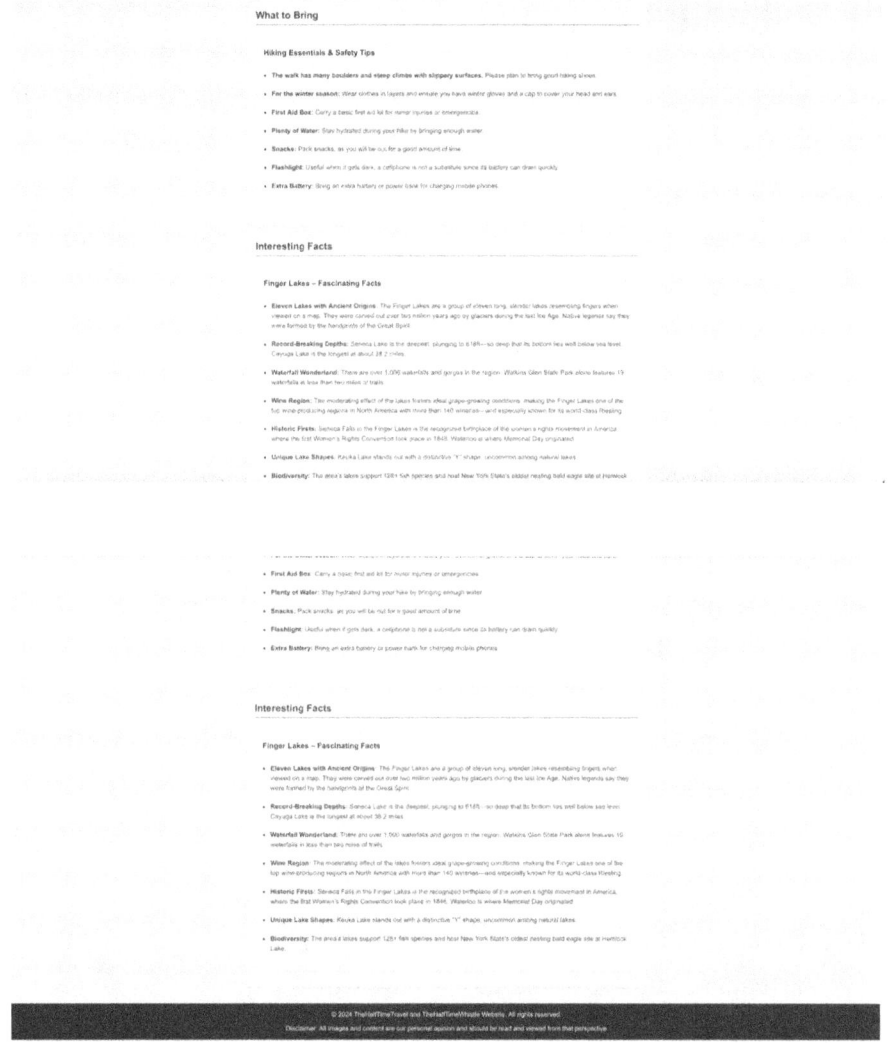

Main Content Display React Page

Let us go through the core modules of the code to understand how the code is structured.

CHAPTER 12   DETAIL TRAVEL PAGE

Imports and Initializations

This section includes the system and application-specific imports and variables required to render the page.

```
import React, { useState, useEffect, useRef } from 'react';
import { useNavigate, useParams, useLocation } from 'react-router-dom';
import DOMPurify from 'dompurify';
import './ContentDisplayOne.css';
import './HomePage.css';
import './ComingSoon.css';

const ContentDisplayOne = () => {
  const navigate = useNavigate();
  const params = useParams();
  const location = useLocation();
  const [region, setRegion] = useState('');
  const [title, setTitle] = useState('');
  const [placeDetails, setPlaceDetails] = useState(null);
  const [isLoading, setIsLoading] = useState(true);
  const [error, setError] = useState(null);
  const carouselRef = useRef(null);
  const [originalTitle, setOriginalTitle] = useState(null);
  const [showPopup, setShowPopup] = useState(false);
  const [popupImages, setPopupImages] = useState([]);
  const [currentImageIndex, setCurrentImageIndex] = useState(0);
```

The following imports are defined

- **React Imports**: Correct usage of React hooks (useState, useEffect, useRef) to perform different React operations.

- **Router Hooks**: Enable the use of useNavigate, useParams, and useLocation for dynamic routing.

- **DOMPurify**: Used for XSS protection when using dangerouslySetInnerHTML.

- **Multiple CSS Imports**: All CSS that we need to render the page.

A set of variables is defined for navigation, parameter usage (title and region to uniquely identify the page content), an object to store all page details returned as a JSON object, carousel details, an error, and a Boolean variable to see if loading is complete.

Retrieve Parameters Function

In this section, we will explore a React functional component using the useEffect hook to retrieve the title and region passed from the previous page as either a URL parameter or a state variable.

The key variables and functions in this snippet are

- **params**: Represents URL parameters for region and title
- **location**: From react-router-dom's useLocation(), representing browser location info
- **setRegion, setTitle, setOriginalTitle**: State setter functions (from useState)
- **originalTitle**: State variable holding the original title

```
useEffect(() => {
    let newRegion = '';
    let newTitle = '';
    if (params.region && params.title) {
      newRegion = decodeURIComponent(params.region);
      newTitle = decodeURIComponent(params.title);
    } else if (location.state && location.state.region && location.state.title) {
      newRegion = location.state.region;
      newTitle = location.state.title;
    } else if (location.pathname) {
      const pathParts = location.pathname.split('/').filter(Boolean);
      if (pathParts.length >= 2) {
        newRegion = decodeURIComponent(pathParts[pathParts.length - 2]);
        newTitle = decodeURIComponent(pathParts[pathParts.length - 1]);
      }
    }
```

```
setRegion(newRegion);
setTitle(newTitle);
if (!originalTitle) {
  setOriginalTitle(newTitle);
}
}, [params.region, params.title, location.state, location.pathname]);
```

The following is a detailed explanation of the code:

- useEffect is a side effect that runs when its dependency array (the last argument) changes.
- Initializes local variables to empty strings. These will store the region and title to be derived from the params.
- If both region and title are present in params (i.e., both are truthy), we
  - Assign their value after decodeURIComponent-ing them (this handles URL encoding, e.g., "New%20York" → "New York").
- Second Priority: If the above wasn't true, check if there's location.state (which is a custom React Router object that lets you pass data through navigation) and both region and title are present in it.
  - Assign directly from location.state.
- Third Priority: If neither of the above, and a path exists:
  - Split the path into parts.
  - If there are at least two segments, take the second-to-the-last segment as the region and the last as the title, both after decoding.
- Update the component's state with these new values.
- If originalTitle isn't set yet, initialize it to the current newTitle. This is for navigation purposes (to the previous screen).
- This useEffect will re-run whenever any of the following change:
  - params.region
  - params.title

- location.state
- location.pathname

Fetch Content

In this section, we will explore a React functional component using the useEffect hook to display the travel detail page based on a region and a title selected by the user in the region page.

```
useEffect(() => {
    const fetchPlaceDetails = async () => {
      if (!region || !title) {
        setError('Region or title is missing');
        setIsLoading(false);
        return;
      }
      try {
        const encodedRegion = encodeURIComponent(region);
        const encodedTitle = encodeURIComponent(title);
        const url = `/api/placedetails/${encodedRegion}/${encodedTitle}`;
        const response = await fetch(url);
        if (!response.ok) {
          const errorText = await response.text();
          throw new Error(`HTTP error! status: ${response.status}, message:
          ${errorText}`);
        }
        const data = await response.json();
        setPlaceDetails(data);
        setError(null);
      } catch (e) {
        console.error('Fetch error:', e);
        setError(`Failed to fetch details for ${title} in ${region}. Error:
        ${e.message}`);
      } finally {
        setIsLoading(false);
      }
```

```
    };
    if (region && title) {
      fetchPlaceDetails();
    }
}, [region, title]);
```

The following is the explanation of the code:

- To run the inner code whenever the region or title variables change.

- Usually, region and title are pieces of state (React useState) that represent what place the user is looking at.

- The data fetching is encapsulated in its own async function, since the main callback for useEffect cannot be async directly. Async allows the content to be fetched while the rest of the code can go on performing its function without waiting for it.

- Checks: If either region or title is not present:
  - An error message is set (by calling setError).
  - Loading state is stopped (setIsLoading(false)).
  - The function exits early – no data fetching attempt.

- Encoding Variables: Both region and title are URL-encoded, so any special characters or spaces are properly handled in the API URL.
  - e.g., "New York" → "New%20York"
  - API Call: Uses fetch to make a GET request to /api/placedetails/{region}/{title}

- HTTP Error Handling
  - If the server responds with an error, it reads the error message and throws an error.

- Parse Data and Update State
  - If successful, parses the response as JSON
  - Updates the UI state with the data (setPlaceDetails(data))
  - Clears any old error messages (setError(null))

CHAPTER 12 DETAIL TRAVEL PAGE

- Any errors – network, parsing, or server – are caught:
  - Error is logged to the console.
  - Error message is updated for the user.
- Whether successful or not, mark loading as false, so any loading spinners, etc. turn off.
- Next, it ensures that you only try to fetch when both region and title are present (non-empty). This small guard is defensive; it ensures you don't accidentally fetch with empty parameters.

Variable Initializations

All the variables defined before are initialized in this section.

```
const getImagePath = (imageName) => {
   if (!imageName) return '';
   try {
     return require(`../assets/${imageName}`);
   } catch (err) {
     console.error(`Error loading image: ${imageName}`, err);
     return '';
   }
};

const scrollCarousel = (direction) => {
   if (carouselRef.current) {
     const scrollAmount = direction === 'left' ? -300 : 300;
     carouselRef.current.scrollBy({ left: scrollAmount, behavior: 'smooth' });
   }
};

const handleImageClick = (imageTitle) => {
   const encodedRegion = encodeURIComponent(placeDetails.region);
   const encodedTitle = encodeURIComponent(imageTitle);
```

CHAPTER 12   DETAIL TRAVEL PAGE

```
    navigate(`/content-display-one/${encodedRegion}/${encodedTitle}`, {
    state: { originalTitle: originalTitle || title } });
};

const handleBackClick = () => {
    if (originalTitle && originalTitle !== title) {
       const encodedRegion = encodeURIComponent(region);
       const encodedOriginalTitle = encodeURIComponent(originalTitle);
       navigate(`/content-display-one/${encodedRegion}/${encodedOriginalTit
       le}`, { replace: true });
    } else {
       navigate(-1);
    }
};

const openPopup = (images, startIndex) => {
    setPopupImages(images);
    setCurrentImageIndex(startIndex);
    setShowPopup(true);
};

const closePopup = () => {
    setShowPopup(false);
};

const nextImage = () => {
    setCurrentImageIndex((prevIndex) => (prevIndex + 1) % popupImages.
    length);
};

const prevImage = () => {
    setCurrentImageIndex((prevIndex) => (prevIndex - 1 + popupImages.
    length) % popupImages.length);
};

const handleDayImageClick = (day, imgIndex) => {
    const images = Object.values(day.images);
    openPopup(images, imgIndex);
};
```

CHAPTER 12   DETAIL TRAVEL PAGE

```
if (isLoading) return <div>Loading...</div>;
if (error) return <div style={{color: 'red', padding:
'20px'}}>{error}</div>;
if (!placeDetails) return <div>No details found</div>;
```

Image Path

- Loads an image from the local assets folder at runtime.
- If imageName is missing or false (e.g., empty/null), returns an empty string (so the caller won't show a broken image).
- Tries to dynamically import the image file. If successful, the required image is returned.
- If it fails (e.g., the image doesn't exist), logs the error in the console and returns an empty string.
- This code is used to resolve image paths dynamically for use in <img src={...} /> elements.

Broken images usually lead to distrust, which is why it's important to have a clear image path.

Scroll Carousel

- Scrolls a horizontally scrollable image or content carousel left or right.
- Checks if a ref to the carousel DOM node exists.
- Sets how much to scroll: -300 pixels for left, +300 for right.
- Calls the DOM method scrollBy to scroll horizontally, with a smooth animation.
- Used by UI arrows or buttons for smooth left/right scrolling of a component containing images or content horizontally. This is displayed right on the top of the page, next to the place image, displaying the places the user visited in an itinerary

Handle Image Click

- Navigates to a detailed view for a selected image/title.
- Gets the region from placeDetails and the clicked image's title.
- Encodes both for safe use in URLs.
- Uses a navigation function (navigate from React Router) to move to a new route, passing the region and title as part of the route.
- Also passes along the "originalTitle" as route state for further use. This is to come back to this page post routing if users choose to do so using navigation.
- This is called when you click an image to view more details.

Handle Back Click

- Handles "back" navigation from the current detail view.
- If there was an original title that's different from the current one, navigates directly to that original detail page (using region and originalTitle; replaces the history entry).
- Otherwise, just goes back to the previous route in browser history (navigate(-1)).
- This enables "smart back" navigation – sometimes you want to go directly back to the original item, not just "one step back".

Open Pop-Up for Image Display

- Opens a modal/pop-up to display images in a gallery/carousel style
- Sets the list of images to display in the pop-up/gallery
- Sets which image to start on
- Shows the pop-up by updating state

Close Image Pop-Up

- Closes the pop-up gallery
- Sets state to hide/close the modal

Next and Previous Image Navigation

- Moves to the next or previous image in the pop-up gallery
- nextImage: Increments image index, wraps around to 0 after the last image
- prevImage: Decrements image index, wraps around to the last image if you go back from the first
- Typically hooked to "next" and "previous" buttons in an image pop-up/modal

Handle Image Click

- Opens the pop-up gallery for a set of images, starting on a specific image
  - Gets an array of images for a given set of images
- Calls openPopup to show the modal, starting at the selected image

Conditional Rendering

- Handles loading, error, and empty-data UI states before rendering the main content.
- If the component is still loading data, shows "Loading…".
- If there's an error, shows the error in red text.
- If no details were found, shows "No details found".
- Otherwise, the main component UI will render.

Content Rendition

This section embeds the HTML to render the fetch content in a particular order. All the class names are in the stylesheet, which we will discuss shortly. The following is a high-level summary of the component layout:

- Displays a detailed view for a travel/place region, including images, descriptions, and multiple sections
- Supports navigation with back button and home link

CHAPTER 12 DETAIL TRAVEL PAGE

- Includes an image carousel with smooth scrolling
- Provides rich HTML content safely rendered with sanitization
- Allows clicking images to view them in a full-screen pop-up with navigation.
- Handles loading and image errors gracefully
- Structures content responsively with semantic HTML and CSS classes
- Includes a footer with copyright/disclaimer.

```
return (
    <div>
      <header className="header">
        <nav className="nav-menu">
          <ul className="menu-level-1">
            <li><a href="/">Home</a></li>
          </ul>
        </nav>
      </header>
      <div className="content-display">
        <h1>{region || "Sample"} Region</h1>
        <button onClick={handleBackClick} className="back-button">
          Back to {originalTitle || "Previous"} Page
        </button>
        <div className="place-details">
          <div className="image-container">
            {placeDetails.image && (
              <img src={getImagePath(placeDetails.image)}
              alt={placeDetails.title} className="main-image" />
            )}
            <h1 className="image-title">{placeDetails.title}</h1>
          </div>
          {placeDetails.imageBlock && placeDetails.imageBlock.length
          > 0 && (
            <div className="image-block-carousel">
```

```jsx
        <button onClick={() => scrollCarousel('left')}
          className="carousel-button left">&lt;</button>
        <div className="carousel" ref={carouselRef}>
          {placeDetails.imageBlock.map((item, index) => (
            <div key={index} className="carousel-item">
              <img
                src={getImagePath(item.image)}
                alt={item.title}
                className="carousel-image clickable"
                onClick={() => handleImageClick(item.title)}
              />
              <h3 className="carousel-title">{item.title}</h3>
            </div>
          ))}
        </div>
        <button onClick={() => scrollCarousel('right')}
          className="carousel-button right">&gt;</button>
      </div>
    )}
    <div className="main-description" dangerouslySetInnerHTML={{ __
    html: DOMPurify.sanitize(placeDetails.description) }} />
</div>
{placeDetails.days && placeDetails.days.map((day, index) => (
  <div key={day._id || index} className="day-block">
    <h2>{day.title}</h2>
    <div dangerouslySetInnerHTML={{ __html: DOMPurify.sanitize(day.
    description) }} />
    {day.images && Object.keys(day.images).length > 0 && (
      <div className="image-gallery">
        {Object.values(day.images).map((image, imgIndex) => (
          <img
            key={imgIndex}
            src={getImagePath(image)}
            alt={`Day ${index + 1} - Image ${imgIndex + 1}`}
            onClick={() => handleDayImageClick(day, imgIndex)}
```

```
                    className="clickable"
                    onError={(e) => {
                      console.error(`Failed to load image: ${image}`);
                      e.target.style.display = 'none';
                    }}
                  />
                ))}
              </div>
            )}
          </div>
        ))}
        {placeDetails.commonBlocks && placeDetails.commonBlocks.map((block,
        index) => (
          <div key={block._id || index} className="common-block">
            <h3>{block.title}</h3>
            <div dangerouslySetInnerHTML={{ __html: DOMPurify.
            sanitize(block.description) }} />
          </div>
        ))}
      </div>
      {showPopup && (
        <div className="popup-overlay" onClick={closePopup}>
          <div className="popup-content" onClick={(e) =>
          e.stopPropagation()}>
            <img src={getImagePath(popupImages[currentImageIndex])}
            alt={`Popup image ${currentImageIndex + 1}`} className="popup-
            image" />
            <button className="popup-close"
            onClick={closePopup}>&times;</button>
            <button className="popup-nav prev"
            onClick={prevImage}>&lt;</button>
            <button className="popup-nav next"
            onClick={nextImage}>&gt;</button>
          </div>
        </div>
      )}
```

```
      <footer className="footer">
        <p>&copy; 2024 TheHalfTimeTravel and TheHalfTimeWhistle Website.
        All rights reserved.</p>
        <p>Disclaimer: All images and content are our personal opinion and
        should be read and viewed from that perspective</p>
      </footer>
    </div>
  );
};
```

Header and Navigation

- A simple top navigation header with a link to Home
- Uses semantic HTML (<header>, <nav>) and CSS classes for styling

Content Display Area

- Shows the current region as an <h1> title; falls back to "Sample" if no region is set

Back Button

- A button that triggers the handleBackClick function when clicked (previously explained).
- The button text shows the originalTitle or "Previous" if it's not set.
- Enables smart back navigation.

Place Detail Selection

- Shows the main image for the place if available. Uses a helper getImagePath() to dynamically load the correct image (explained above).
- Displays the place's title below the image.

Image Block Carousel

- If the place has an imageBlock array with images:
  - Renders a horizontal carousel of these images.
  - Left and right buttons call scrollCarousel() to scroll the carousel container smoothly (explained before).

- Each image
  - Uses getImagePath to load its source (explained before).
  - Is clickable: clicking calls handleImageClick with that image's title (explained before).
- Titles shown below each carousel image.

Description Section

- The place's main description is shown here.
- Uses React's dangerouslySetInnerHTML to insert raw HTML.
- The content is sanitized via DOMPurify to prevent XSS security issues.
- This allows rich HTML content for descriptions safely.

Repeating Block with Optional Images

- For each block in placeDetails.days, it renders
  - A block with title and sanitized description
- If the block has images:
  - Shows all images as clickable <img> thumbnails
  - Clicking an image calls handleDayImageClick to open the popup starting with that image. (explained before)
  - Includes error handling for failed image loads (hides broken images and logs errors)

Common Info Blocks

- Renders common blocks of content related to the place (generic info). This is like the main content block but has a different stylesheet class.
- Each has a title and sanitized HTML description.

CHAPTER 12   DETAIL TRAVEL PAGE

Pop-Up Mode for Image Viewing

- When the showPopup state is true, this modal overlays the page.
- Clicking the overlay outside content calls closePopup (to dismiss).
- The pop-up content includes
  - The current pop-up image from popupImages at currentImageIndex
  - Close button (×)
  - Previous < and next > buttons to navigate images inside the pop-up gallery
- Clicks inside the pop-up content do not propagate to the overlay, preventing accidental close while interacting.

Footer

- Simple footer at the bottom of the page.
- Contains copyright and a disclaimer.

Complete Code

Here is the complete code of the React page.

```
import React, { useState, useEffect, useRef } from 'react';
import { useNavigate, useParams, useLocation } from 'react-router-dom';
import DOMPurify from 'dompurify';
import './ContentDisplayOne.css';
import './HomePage.css';
import './ComingSoon.css';

const ContentDisplayOne = () => {
  const navigate = useNavigate();
  const params = useParams();
  const location = useLocation();
  const [region, setRegion] = useState('');
  const [title, setTitle] = useState('');
  const [placeDetails, setPlaceDetails] = useState(null);
```

```
  const [isLoading, setIsLoading] = useState(true);
  const [error, setError] = useState(null);
  const carouselRef = useRef(null);
  const [originalTitle, setOriginalTitle] = useState(null);
  const [showPopup, setShowPopup] = useState(false);
  const [popupImages, setPopupImages] = useState([]);
  const [currentImageIndex, setCurrentImageIndex] = useState(0);

useEffect(() => {
  let newRegion = '';
  let newTitle = '';
  if (params.region && params.title) {
    newRegion = decodeURIComponent(params.region);
    newTitle = decodeURIComponent(params.title);
  } else if (location.state && location.state.region && location.state.
  title) {
    newRegion = location.state.region;
    newTitle = location.state.title;
  } else if (location.pathname) {
    const pathParts = location.pathname.split('/').filter(Boolean);
    if (pathParts.length >= 2) {
      newRegion = decodeURIComponent(pathParts[pathParts.length - 2]);
      newTitle = decodeURIComponent(pathParts[pathParts.length - 1]);
    }
  }
  setRegion(newRegion);
  setTitle(newTitle);
  if (!originalTitle) {
    setOriginalTitle(newTitle);
  }
}, [params.region, params.title, location.state, location.pathname]);

useEffect(() => {
  const fetchPlaceDetails = async () => {
    if (!region || !title) {
      setError('Region or title is missing');
```

```
      setIsLoading(false);
      return;
    }
    try {
      const encodedRegion = encodeURIComponent(region);
      const encodedTitle = encodeURIComponent(title);
      const url = `/api/placedetails/${encodedRegion}/${encodedTitle}`;
      const response = await fetch(url);
      if (!response.ok) {
        const errorText = await response.text();
        throw new Error(`HTTP error! status: ${response.status}, message:
        ${errorText}`);
      }
      const data = await response.json();
      setPlaceDetails(data);
      setError(null);
    } catch (e) {
      console.error('Fetch error:', e);
      setError(`Failed to fetch details for ${title} in ${region}. Error:
      ${e.message}`);
    } finally {
      setIsLoading(false);
    }
  };
  if (region && title) {
    fetchPlaceDetails();
  }
}, [region, title]);

const getImagePath = (imageName) => {
  if (!imageName) return '';
  try {
    return require(`../assets/${imageName}`);
  } catch (err) {
    console.error(`Error loading image: ${imageName}`, err);
    return '';
```

```
    }
  };

  const scrollCarousel = (direction) => {
    if (carouselRef.current) {
      const scrollAmount = direction === 'left' ? -300 : 300;
      carouselRef.current.scrollBy({ left: scrollAmount, behavior:
      'smooth' });
    }
  };

  const handleImageClick = (imageTitle) => {
    const encodedRegion = encodeURIComponent(placeDetails.region);
    const encodedTitle = encodeURIComponent(imageTitle);
    navigate(`/content-display-one/${encodedRegion}/${encodedTitle}`, {
    state: { originalTitle: originalTitle || title } });
  };

  const handleBackClick = () => {
    if (originalTitle && originalTitle !== title) {
      const encodedRegion = encodeURIComponent(region);
      const encodedOriginalTitle = encodeURIComponent(originalTitle);
      navigate(`/content-display-one/${encodedRegion}/${encodedOriginalTit
      le}`, { replace: true });
    } else {
      navigate(-1);
    }
  };

  const openPopup = (images, startIndex) => {
    setPopupImages(images);
    setCurrentImageIndex(startIndex);
    setShowPopup(true);
  };

  const closePopup = () => {
    setShowPopup(false);
  };
```

```
  const nextImage = () => {
    setCurrentImageIndex((prevIndex) => (prevIndex + 1) % popupImages.
    length);
  };

  const prevImage = () => {
    setCurrentImageIndex((prevIndex) => (prevIndex - 1 + popupImages.
    length) % popupImages.length);
  };

  const handleDayImageClick = (day, imgIndex) => {
    const images = Object.values(day.images);
    openPopup(images, imgIndex);
  };

  if (isLoading) return <div>Loading...</div>;
  if (error) return <div style={{color: 'red', padding:
'20px'}}>{error}</div>;
  if (!placeDetails) return <div>No details found</div>;

  return (
    <div>
      <header className="header">
        <nav className="nav-menu">
          <ul className="menu-level-1">
            <li><a href="/">Home</a></li>
          </ul>
        </nav>
      </header>
      <div className="content-display">
        <h1>{region || "Sample"} Region</h1>
        <button onClick={handleBackClick} className="back-button">
          Back to {originalTitle || "Previous"} Page
        </button>
        <div className="place-details">
          <div className="image-container">
            {placeDetails.image && (
```

```jsx
        <img src={getImagePath(placeDetails.image)}
        alt={placeDetails.title} className="main-image" />
      )}
      <h1 className="image-title">{placeDetails.title}</h1>
    </div>
    {placeDetails.imageBlock && placeDetails.imageBlock.length
    > 0 && (
      <div className="image-block-carousel">
        <button onClick={() => scrollCarousel('left')}
        className="carousel-button left">&lt;</button>
        <div className="carousel" ref={carouselRef}>
          {placeDetails.imageBlock.map((item, index) => (
            <div key={index} className="carousel-item">
              <img
                src={getImagePath(item.image)}
                alt={item.title}
                className="carousel-image clickable"
                onClick={() => handleImageClick(item.title)}
              />
              <h3 className="carousel-title">{item.title}</h3>
            </div>
          ))}
        </div>
        <button onClick={() => scrollCarousel('right')}
        className="carousel-button right">&gt;</button>
      </div>
    )}
    <div className="main-description" dangerouslySetInnerHTML={{ __
    html: DOMPurify.sanitize(placeDetails.description) }} />
  </div>
  {placeDetails.days && placeDetails.days.map((day, index) => (
    <div key={day._id || index} className="day-block">
      <h2>{day.title}</h2>
      <div dangerouslySetInnerHTML={{ __html: DOMPurify.sanitize(day.
      description) }} />
```

```
      {day.images && Object.keys(day.images).length > 0 && (
        <div className="image-gallery">
          {Object.values(day.images).map((image, imgIndex) => (
            <img
              key={imgIndex}
              src={getImagePath(image)}
              alt={`Day ${index + 1} - Image ${imgIndex + 1}`}
              onClick={() => handleDayImageClick(day, imgIndex)}
              className="clickable"
              onError={(e) => {
                console.error(`Failed to load image: ${image}`);
                e.target.style.display = 'none';
              }}
            />
          ))}
        </div>
      )}
    </div>
  ))}
  {placeDetails.commonBlocks && placeDetails.commonBlocks.map((block,
  index) => (
    <div key={block._id || index} className="common-block">
      <h3>{block.title}</h3>
      <div dangerouslySetInnerHTML={{ __html: DOMPurify.
      sanitize(block.description) }} />
    </div>
  ))}
</div>
{showPopup && (
  <div className="popup-overlay" onClick={closePopup}>
    <div className="popup-content" onClick={(e) =>
    e.stopPropagation()}>
      <img src={getImagePath(popupImages[currentImageIndex])}
      alt={`Popup image ${currentImageIndex + 1}`} className="popup-
      image" />
```

CHAPTER 12 DETAIL TRAVEL PAGE

```
              <button className="popup-close"
              onClick={closePopup}>&times;</button>
              <button className="popup-nav prev"
              onClick={prevImage}>&lt;</button>
              <button className="popup-nav next"
              onClick={nextImage}>&gt;</button>
            </div>
          </div>
        )}
        <footer className="footer">
          <p>&copy; 2024 TheHalfTimeTravel and TheHalfTimeWhistle Website.
          All rights reserved.</p>
          <p>Disclaimer: All images and content are our personal opinion and
          should be read and viewed from that perspective</p>
        </footer>
      </div>
    );
  };

export default ContentDisplayOne;
```

AI Prompt

You can use the following detailed AI prompt to generate the code.

Prompt

Generate a complete React functional component named ContentDisplayOne that meets the following specifications:

- Uses React hooks: useState, useEffect, and useRef.

- Utilizes React Router hooks: useNavigate, useParams, and useLocation.

- Imports the DOMPurify library to sanitize HTML content before rendering.

- Imports three CSS files: './ContentDisplayOne.css', './HomePage.css', and './ComingSoon.css'.

- Manages state variables: region, title, placeDetails, isLoading, error, originalTitle, showPopup, popupImages, and currentImageIndex.

- Uses a carouselRef with useRef for the image carousel.

- Extracts region and title from URL parameters, location state, or pathname segments using useEffect.

- Fetches JSON place details from an API endpoint /api/placedetails/{region}/{title} where region and title are URL-encoded.

- Implements error handling and loading state during data fetching.

- Defines a getImagePath helper function that tries to dynamically require images from the ../assets/ folder and returns an empty string on failure.

- Implements carousel scrolling functions to scroll left or right smoothly by 300 pixels.

- Defines click handlers to navigate to other content, handle back navigation, open and close an image popup, and paginate images inside the popup.

- Renders:
    - A header with a home navigation link.
    - The region title.
    - A back button that either goes back to the original title page or browser history.
    - Place details including main image, title, a carousel of images with clickable items, and sanitized description HTML.
    - Day blocks with titles, sanitized descriptions, and clickable image galleries that open a popup.
    - Common blocks with titles and sanitized HTML descriptions.
    - A popup image overlay with navigation and close buttons.
    - A footer with copyright and disclaimer text.

CHAPTER 12   DETAIL TRAVEL PAGE

- Adds relevant CSS classNames on elements as per the original code.
- Handles image onError inside galleries by hiding the broken image and logging an error.
- Uses dangerouslySetInnerHTML only with sanitized HTML via DOMPurify.sanitize.
- All navigation is done with React Router's navigate function.
- Exports the component as default.

Ensure the code syntax, structure, and logic exactly match the provided component, including use of all hooks, event handlers, state management, conditional renderings, and inline styles for errors.

Stylesheet

The file uses some style from HomePage.css and Region.css file (ItemStyle.css) as the header and core layout are the same. There are some unique styles like the common block, the image carousel, and the image pop-up, which need some special treatment and are mentioned in this stylesheet.

Root

```
:root {
  --color-text: #333;
  --color-link: #0066cc;
  --color-bg: #f0f0f0;
  --color-bg-main-description: #ffffff;
  --color-bg-day-block: #f9f9f9;
  --color-bg-common-block: #e8f4f8;
  --color-shadow: 0 2px 4px rgba(0,0,0,0.1);
  --color-shadow-block: 0 2px 5px rgba(0,0,0,0.1);
  --color-heading: #2c3e50;
  --color-border-heading: #3498db;
  --color-heading-common-block: #2980b9;
  --color-link-dining: #0066cc;
```

CHAPTER 12   DETAIL TRAVEL PAGE

```css
  --color-popup-bg: rgba(0, 0, 0, 0.8);
  --color-popup-button: rgba(0, 0, 0, 0.5);
  --color-image-title-bg: rgba(0, 0, 0, 0.7);

  --ff-base: 'Segoe UI', Arial, sans-serif;

  /* Spacing scale */
  --space-0: 0;
  --space-1: 0.25rem;
  --space-2: 0.5rem;
  --space-3: 1rem;
  --space-4: 1.5rem;
  --space-5: 2rem;
  --space-6: 2.5rem;
}
```

Using the .root selector for defining the centralized theme and spacing. This makes the stylesheet easy to maintain and scalable.

Utility Spacing

```css
/* Utility spacing classes */
.mb-10 { margin-bottom: var(--space-3) !important; }
.mb-20 { margin-bottom: var(--space-5) !important; }
.mt-10 { margin-top: var(--space-3) !important; }
.pt-10 { padding-top: var(--space-3) !important; }
.pt-20 { padding-top: var(--space-5) !important; }
.pb-10 { padding-bottom: var(--space-3) !important; }
.pb-20 { padding-bottom: var(--space-5) !important; }
```

This defines CSS utility classes that control margin and padding spacing on elements by applying specific properties with consistent values derived from CSS variables.

CHAPTER 12   DETAIL TRAVEL PAGE

Body, Heading, and Paragraph Styling

```css
body {
  font-family: var(--ff-base);
  line-height: 1.5;
  color: var(--color-text);
  max-width: 100%;
  margin: 0 auto;
  padding: var(--space-2);
  background-color: var(--color-bg);
  font-size: 1rem;
}

/* Responsive text scaling */
@media (max-width: 768px) {
  body {
    padding: var(--space-1);
    font-size: 0.95rem;
  }
}

h1, h2, h3, h4, h5, h6 {
  margin-block: var(--space-0) var(--space-0);
}

p {
  margin-block: var(--space-3);
  line-height: 1.5;
}
```

body

- Uses Arial or a Sans Serif font
- Sets line height to 1 (single spacing)
- Dark gray text color (#333)

- Limits width to 100% and centers content horizontally (margin: 0 auto)
- Adds 10px padding and a light gray background (#f0f0f0)

Headings (h1 to h6)

- Very small vertical margins (1px top and bottom) for tight spacing

Paragraphs (p)

- 10px top and bottom margins, line height increased to 1.5 for readability

List Styling

```
.park-info p {
  margin-block-end: var(--space-3);
}

ul, ol {
  margin-block: var(--space-0);
  padding-inline-start: var(--space-5);
  padding-inline-end: var(--space-0);
}

li {
  margin-block-end: var(--space-1);
}

a {
  color: var(--color-link);
  text-decoration: none;
  outline: none;
}

a:focus, .back-button:focus, .carousel-button:focus, .popup-close:focus,
.popup-nav:focus {
  outline: 2px dashed var(--color-link);
```

```css
  outline-offset: 2px;
  background: #e2eefd;
}
a:hover {
  text-decoration: underline;
}
a[aria-label] {
  /* Suggest that all navigation/semantic anchors get ARIA labels */
}
```

Lists (ul, ol)

- Small vertical margins (1px top and bottom), left padding for list markers

List items (li)

- Small bottom margin (1px)

Links (a)

- Blue color (#0066cc), no underline initially, underline on hover

Layout and Containers

```css
.content-display {
  max-width: 62.5rem;
  margin-inline: auto;
  padding: var(--space-5);
}
.back-button {
  background-color: var(--color-bg);
  border: none;
  padding: var(--space-2) var(--space-3);
  margin-block-end: var(--space-5);
  cursor: pointer;
  border-radius: var(--space-1);
```

```css
  transition: background 0.2s;
}

.back-button:focus {
  outline: 2px solid var(--color-link);
}

.main-title {
  font-size: 2.5rem;
  color: var(--color-text);
}

.main-description {
  font-size: 1.1rem;
  line-height: 1.6;
  color: #666;
  background-color: var(--color-bg-main-description);
  border-radius: var(--space-2);
  box-shadow: var(--color-shadow);
  margin: 0;
  padding: var(--space-5);
  font-family: var(--ff-base);
}

.day-block {
  background-color: var(--color-bg-day-block);
  border-radius: var(--space-3);
  padding: var(--space-5);
  margin-block: var(--space-5);
  box-shadow: var(--color-shadow-block);
  font-family: var(--ff-base);
}

.day-block h2 {
  color: var(--color-heading);
  border-bottom: 2px solid var(--color-border-heading);
  padding-block-end: var(--space-3);
}
```

```
.day-block ul,
.day-block ol {
  margin-block: var(--space-3);
}

.day-block li {
  margin-block-end: var(--space-2);
  line-height: 1.5;
}

.day-block li > ul,
.day-block li > ol {
  margin-block: var(--space-2);
}
```

.content-display

Max width 1000px centered with auto margins, padding 20px.

.back-button

Light gray background, no border, some padding, bottom margin, pointer cursor, and rounded corners.

.main-title

Large font size (2.5em), dark text color (#333).

.main-description

Slightly bigger font (1.1em), line height 1.6 for easy reading, lighter color (#666), white background, rounded corners, subtle box shadow, 20px padding.

.day-block

Light background (#f9f9f9), rounded with padding, margin spacing, and subtle shadows.

Its h2 headings have a colored bottom border and padding.

Lists Inside .day-block

Extra margin around lists within day blocks to separate the items visually.

Image Gallery

```
image-gallery {
  display: grid;
  grid-template-columns: repeat(auto-fit, minmax(12.5rem, 1fr));
```

```css
  gap: var(--space-3);
  margin-block-start: var(--space-5);
}

.image-gallery img {
  width: 100%;
  height: 12.5rem;
  object-fit: cover;
  border-radius: var(--space-1);
  box-shadow: var(--color-shadow);
}

.image-gallery img[aria-hidden="true"] {
  /* Decorative images */
  pointer-events: none;
}
```

Uses a CSS grid with columns that auto-fit and have a minimum size of 200px.

Images have fixed height (200px), cover cropping, rounded corners, and subtle shadow.

This displays all images in a grid on the main page.

Common Blocks

```css
.common-block {
  background-color: var(--color-bg-common-block);
  border-radius: var(--space-3);
  padding: var(--space-5);
  margin-block: var(--space-5);
  box-shadow: var(--color-shadow-block);
  font-family: var(--ff-base);
}

.common-block h2 {
  color: var(--color-heading-common-block);
  border-bottom: 2px solid var(--color-border-heading);
  padding-block-end: var(--space-3);
}
```

This is the common block, which is a little different from the main block as it has a blue background. This is usually used as an end block to display miscellaneous content.

Background color is light blue (#e8f4f8), rounded corners, padding, margin, and a box shadow similar to .day-block.

Section-Specific Styles

```
travel-log,
.day-itinerary,
.park-entry-info,
.accommodation-info,
.dining-guide,
.packing-list,
.park-info {
  margin-block-end: var(--space-0);
}

.travel-log h2,
.day-itinerary h2,
.park-entry-info h2,
.accommodation-info h2,
.dining-guide h2,
.park-info h2 {
  border-bottom: 1px solid var(--color-text);
  padding-block-end: var(--space-1);
  margin-block-end: var(--space-0);
}

.park-entry-info ul,
.accommodation-info ol,
.dining-guide ul {
  margin-block-end: var(--space-0);
}

.accommodation-info ol > li {
  margin-block-end: var(--space-0);
}
```

```css
.dining-guide h3 {
  margin-block: var(--space-0);
  color: var(--color-link-dining);
}

.dining-guide > ul {
  margin-block: var(--space-0);
}

.dining-guide > ul > li {
  margin-block-end: var(--space-0);
}

.dining-guide > ul > li:last-child {
  margin-block-end: var(--space-0);
}

.dining-guide ul ul {
  margin-block: var(--space-0);
}
.dining-guide ul ul li {
  margin-block-end: var(--space-0);
}

.packing-list ol {
  list-style-type: disc;
  margin-block-end: 0.5rem;
  padding-inline-start: var(--space-5);
}

.packing-list li {
  margin-block-end: 0.5rem;
  line-height: 1.5;
}
```

.travel-log, .day-itinerary, .park-entry-info, and accommodations have small bottom margins.

Their h2 headers have bottom borders and spacing for separation.

For Dining-Specific Ones
h3 headings in dining-guide are blue and have small margins.
Lists and nested lists have consistent small margins for neatness.
Packing List
Uses disc-style lists, small bottom margins, and a slightly larger line height.

Image Styling

```
.image-container {
  position: relative;
  width: 100%;
  max-width: 62.5rem;
  margin-inline: auto;
  overflow: hidden;
  padding-top: 50%;
}

.image-container img[aria-hidden="true"] {
  /* Decorative images, skip accessibility tree */
  pointer-events: none;
}

.image-container img {
  width: 100%;
  height: 110%;
  object-fit: cover;
  object-position: center;
}

.main-image {
  position: absolute;
  top: 0;
  left: 0;
  width: 100%;
  height: 100%;
```

```css
  object-fit: cover;
  object-position: center top;
}

.image-title {
  position: absolute;
  bottom: 0;
  left: 0;
  right: 0;
  background-color: var(--color-image-title-bg);
  color: white;
  padding: var(--space-3);
  margin: 0;
  font-size: 1.5rem;
  text-align: center;
}

.place-details {
  display: flex;
  flex-direction: column;
  align-items: center;
  width: 100%;
}

.strong {
  font-weight: bold;
}

.emphasis {
  font-style: italic;
}
/* ---------------------------------
   Carousel & Popups
---------------------------------- */
.image-block-carousel {
  position: relative;
  width: 100%;
```

```css
  margin-block: var(--space-5);
  overflow: hidden;
}

.carousel {
  display: flex;
  overflow-x: auto;
  scroll-snap-type: x mandatory;
  -webkit-overflow-scrolling: touch;
  scrollbar-width: none;
  -ms-overflow-style: none;
  padding-block: var(--space-2);
}

.carousel::-webkit-scrollbar {
  display: none;
}

.carousel-item {
  flex: 0 0 auto;
  width: 12.5rem;
  margin-inline-end: var(--space-5);
  scroll-snap-align: start;
  display: flex;
  flex-direction: column;
  align-items: center;
}

.carousel-image {
  width: 100%;
  height: 9.375rem;
  object-fit: cover;
  border-radius: var(--space-2);
}

.carousel-title {
  margin-block-start: var(--space-3);
  font-size: 0.875rem;
```

```css
  text-align: center;
  max-width: 100%;
}

.carousel-button {
  position: absolute;
  top: 50%;
  transform: translateY(-50%);
  background-color: var(--color-popup-button);
  color: white;
  border: none;
  padding: var(--space-3);
  cursor: pointer;
  font-size: 1.125rem;
  z-index: 10;
  border-radius: 50%;
  transition: background 0.2s;
}

.carousel-button:focus {
  outline: 2px solid var(--color-link);
}

.carousel-button.left {
  left: var(--space-3);
}

.carousel-button.right {
  right: var(--space-3);
}

.carousel-image.clickable {
  pointer-events: auto !important;
  cursor: pointer !important;
}

.clickable {
  cursor: pointer;
}
```

```css
.popup-overlay {
  position: fixed;
  top: 0;
  left: 0;
  right: 0;
  bottom: 0;
  background-color: var(--color-popup-bg);
  display: flex;
  justify-content: center;
  align-items: center;
  z-index: 1000;
}

.popup-content {
  position: relative;
  max-width: 90%;
  max-height: 90%;
}

.popup-image {
  max-width: 100%;
  max-height: 90vh;
  object-fit: contain;
}

.popup-close {
  position: absolute;
  top: var(--space-3);
  right: var(--space-3);
  background: none;
  border: none;
  color: white;
  font-size: 1.5rem;
  cursor: pointer;
  transition: color 0.2s;
}
```

```css
.popup-close:focus {
  outline: 2px solid var(--color-link);
}

.popup-nav {
  position: absolute;
  top: 50%;
  transform: translateY(-50%);
  background: var(--color-popup-button);
  color: white;
  border: none;
  padding: var(--space-3);
  font-size: 1.125rem;
  cursor: pointer;
}
.popup-nav:focus {
  outline: 2px solid var(--color-link);
}

.popup-nav.prev {
  left: var(--space-3);
}

.popup-nav.next {
  right: var(--space-3);
}

@media (max-width: 768px) {
  .image-title {
    font-size: 1.2rem;
  }
  .image-gallery {
    grid-template-columns: repeat(auto-fit, minmax(9.375rem, 1fr));
  }
  .image-gallery img {
    height: 9.375rem;
  }
```

```css
  .dining-guide p {
    margin-block-end: var(--space-0);
  }
  .carousel-item {
    width: 9.375rem;
  }
  .carousel-image {
    height: 6.25rem;
  }
  .carousel-title {
    font-size: 0.75rem;
  }
  .popup-content {
    width: 95%;
  }
  .popup-nav {
    padding: var(--space-1);
    font-size: 1rem;
  }
}

/* Accessibility enhancement for ARIA labels and focus */
[aria-label] {
  cursor: pointer;
}
```

Image Container

Uses a relative container with padding-top to maintain aspect ratio (50% padding-top forms a 2:1 ratio container).

Images inside are positioned absolutely to cover the container area, maintaining focus in the center or top.

Text Classes

.strong forces bold text.

.emphasis forces italic text.

Carousel Styles

.image-block-carousel is a container with overflow hidden and a relative position.

.carousel uses flexbox with horizontal scrolling and snap points for smooth scrolling on touch devices.

Scrollbar is hidden across browsers.

.carousel-item specifies fixed-width items aligned vertically with an image and title below.

Navigation buttons positioned on left/right sides with semi-transparent background circles and large font.

Clickable Elements

.clickable cursor turns to a pointer for user interaction indication.

Pop-Up Overlay for Lightbox Images

Full-screen fixed overlay with semi-transparent black background.

Content centered (image and controls).

Image scaled to a max height/width within the viewport.

Close button in the top right corner in white.

Navigation arrows on the sides.

Responsive Styles (@media max-width 600px)

Reduce padding on the body.

Smaller font sizes for image titles and carousel titles.

Image gallery columns shrink to at least 150px wide.

Image heights reduced for gallery and carousel.

Pop-up elements are sized smaller, and navigation buttons are smaller for mobile usage.

Complete Code

```
:root {
  --color-text: #333;
  --color-link: #0066cc;
  --color-bg: #f0f0f0;
  --color-bg-main-description: #ffffff;
  --color-bg-day-block: #f9f9f9;
  --color-bg-common-block: #e8f4f8;
  --color-shadow: 0 2px 4px rgba(0,0,0,0.1);
  --color-shadow-block: 0 2px 5px rgba(0,0,0,0.1);
  --color-heading: #2c3e50;
  --color-border-heading: #3498db;
```

```css
  --color-heading-common-block: #2980b9;
  --color-link-dining: #0066cc;
  --color-popup-bg: rgba(0, 0, 0, 0.8);
  --color-popup-button: rgba(0, 0, 0, 0.5);
  --color-image-title-bg: rgba(0, 0, 0, 0.7);

  --ff-base: 'Segoe UI', Arial, sans-serif;

  /* Spacing scale */
  --space-0: 0;
  --space-1: 0.25rem;
  --space-2: 0.5rem;
  --space-3: 1rem;
  --space-4: 1.5rem;
  --space-5: 2rem;
  --space-6: 2.5rem;
}

/* Utility spacing classes */
.mb-10 { margin-bottom: var(--space-3) !important; }
.mb-20 { margin-bottom: var(--space-5) !important; }
.mt-10 { margin-top: var(--space-3) !important; }
.pt-10 { padding-top: var(--space-3) !important; }
.pt-20 { padding-top: var(--space-5) !important; }
.pb-10 { padding-bottom: var(--space-3) !important; }
.pb-20 { padding-bottom: var(--space-5) !important; }

body {
  font-family: var(--ff-base);
  line-height: 1.5;
  color: var(--color-text);
  max-width: 100%;
  margin: 0 auto;
  padding: var(--space-2);
  background-color: var(--color-bg);
  font-size: 1rem;
}
```

```css
/* Responsive text scaling */
@media (max-width: 768px) {
  body {
    padding: var(--space-1);
    font-size: 0.95rem;
  }
}

h1, h2, h3, h4, h5, h6 {
  margin-block: var(--space-0) var(--space-0);
}

p {
  margin-block: var(--space-3);
  line-height: 1.5;
}

.park-info p {
  margin-block-end: var(--space-3);
}

ul, ol {
  margin-block: var(--space-0);
  padding-inline-start: var(--space-5);
  padding-inline-end: var(--space-0);
}

li {
  margin-block-end: var(--space-1);
}

a {
  color: var(--color-link);
  text-decoration: none;
  outline: none;
}

a:focus, .back-button:focus, .carousel-button:focus, .popup-close:focus,
.popup-nav:focus {
```

```css
    outline: 2px dashed var(--color-link);
    outline-offset: 2px;
    background: #e2eefd;
}

a:hover {
    text-decoration: underline;
}

a[aria-label] {
    /* Suggest that all navigation/semantic anchors get ARIA labels */
}

.content-display {
    max-width: 62.5rem;
    margin-inline: auto;
    padding: var(--space-5);
}

.back-button {
    background-color: var(--color-bg);
    border: none;
    padding: var(--space-2) var(--space-3);
    margin-block-end: var(--space-5);
    cursor: pointer;
    border-radius: var(--space-1);
    transition: background 0.2s;
}

.back-button:focus {
    outline: 2px solid var(--color-link);
}

.main-title {
    font-size: 2.5rem;
    color: var(--color-text);
}
```

```css
.main-description {
  font-size: 1.1rem;
  line-height: 1.6;
  color: #666;
  background-color: var(--color-bg-main-description);
  border-radius: var(--space-2);
  box-shadow: var(--color-shadow);
  margin: 0;
  padding: var(--space-5);
  font-family: var(--ff-base);
}

.day-block {
  background-color: var(--color-bg-day-block);
  border-radius: var(--space-3);
  padding: var(--space-5);
  margin-block: var(--space-5);
  box-shadow: var(--color-shadow-block);
  font-family: var(--ff-base);
}

.day-block h2 {
  color: var(--color-heading);
  border-bottom: 2px solid var(--color-border-heading);
  padding-block-end: var(--space-3);
}

.day-block ul,
.day-block ol {
  margin-block: var(--space-3);
}

.day-block li {
  margin-block-end: var(--space-2);
  line-height: 1.5;
}
```

```css
.day-block li > ul,
.day-block li > ol {
  margin-block: var(--space-2);
}

.image-gallery {
  display: grid;
  grid-template-columns: repeat(auto-fit, minmax(12.5rem, 1fr));
  gap: var(--space-3);
  margin-block-start: var(--space-5);
}

.image-gallery img {
  width: 100%;
  height: 12.5rem;
  object-fit: cover;
  border-radius: var(--space-1);
  box-shadow: var(--color-shadow);
}

.image-gallery img[aria-hidden="true"] {
  /* Decorative images */
  pointer-events: none;
}

.common-block {
  background-color: var(--color-bg-common-block);
  border-radius: var(--space-3);
  padding: var(--space-5);
  margin-block: var(--space-5);
  box-shadow: var(--color-shadow-block);
  font-family: var(--ff-base);
}

.common-block h2 {
  color: var(--color-heading-common-block);
  border-bottom: 2px solid var(--color-border-heading);
  padding-block-end: var(--space-3);
```

```css
}

.travel-log,
.day-itinerary,
.park-entry-info,
.accommodation-info,
.dining-guide,
.packing-list,
.park-info {
  margin-block-end: var(--space-0);
}

.travel-log h2,
.day-itinerary h2,
.park-entry-info h2,
.accommodation-info h2,
.dining-guide h2,
.park-info h2 {
  border-bottom: 1px solid var(--color-text);
  padding-block-end: var(--space-1);
  margin-block-end: var(--space-0);
}

.park-entry-info ul,
.accommodation-info ol,
.dining-guide ul {
  margin-block-end: var(--space-0);
}

.accommodation-info ol > li {
  margin-block-end: var(--space-0);
}

.dining-guide h3 {
  margin-block: var(--space-0);
  color: var(--color-link-dining);
}
```

```css
.dining-guide > ul {
  margin-block: var(--space-0);
}

.dining-guide > ul > li {
  margin-block-end: var(--space-0);
}

.dining-guide > ul > li:last-child {
  margin-block-end: var(--space-0);
}

.dining-guide ul ul {
  margin-block: var(--space-0);
}
.dining-guide ul ul li {
  margin-block-end: var(--space-0);
}

.packing-list ol {
  list-style-type: disc;
  margin-block-end: 0.5rem;
  padding-inline-start: var(--space-5);
}

.packing-list li {
  margin-block-end: 0.5rem;
  line-height: 1.5;
}

.image-container {
  position: relative;
  width: 100%;
  max-width: 62.5rem;
  margin-inline: auto;
  overflow: hidden;
  padding-top: 50%;
}
```

```css
.image-container img[aria-hidden="true"] {
  /* Decorative images, skip accessibility tree */
  pointer-events: none;
}

.image-container img {
  width: 100%;
  height: 110%;
  object-fit: cover;
  object-position: center;
}

.main-image {
  position: absolute;
  top: 0;
  left: 0;
  width: 100%;
  height: 100%;
  object-fit: cover;
  object-position: center top;
}

.image-title {
  position: absolute;
  bottom: 0;
  left: 0;
  right: 0;
  background-color: var(--color-image-title-bg);
  color: white;
  padding: var(--space-3);
  margin: 0;
  font-size: 1.5rem;
  text-align: center;
}

.place-details {
  display: flex;
```

```css
    flex-direction: column;
    align-items: center;
    width: 100%;
  }

  .strong {
    font-weight: bold;
  }

  .emphasis {
    font-style: italic;
  }
  /* --------------------------------
     Carousel & Popups
     -------------------------------- */
  .image-block-carousel {
    position: relative;
    width: 100%;
    margin-block: var(--space-5);
    overflow: hidden;
  }

  .carousel {
    display: flex;
    overflow-x: auto;
    scroll-snap-type: x mandatory;
    -webkit-overflow-scrolling: touch;
    scrollbar-width: none;
    -ms-overflow-style: none;
    padding-block: var(--space-2);
  }

  .carousel::-webkit-scrollbar {
    display: none;
  }
```

```css
.carousel-item {
  flex: 0 0 auto;
  width: 12.5rem;
  margin-inline-end: var(--space-5);
  scroll-snap-align: start;
  display: flex;
  flex-direction: column;
  align-items: center;
}

.carousel-image {
  width: 100%;
  height: 9.375rem;
  object-fit: cover;
  border-radius: var(--space-2);
}

.carousel-title {
  margin-block-start: var(--space-3);
  font-size: 0.875rem;
  text-align: center;
  max-width: 100%;
}

.carousel-button {
  position: absolute;
  top: 50%;
  transform: translateY(-50%);
  background-color: var(--color-popup-button);
  color: white;
  border: none;
  padding: var(--space-3);
  cursor: pointer;
  font-size: 1.125rem;
  z-index: 10;
```

```css
  border-radius: 50%;
  transition: background 0.2s;
}

.carousel-button:focus {
  outline: 2px solid var(--color-link);
}

.carousel-button.left {
  left: var(--space-3);
}

.carousel-button.right {
  right: var(--space-3);
}

.carousel-image.clickable {
  pointer-events: auto !important;
  cursor: pointer !important;
}

.clickable {
  cursor: pointer;
}

.popup-overlay {
  position: fixed;
  top: 0;
  left: 0;
  right: 0;
  bottom: 0;
  background-color: var(--color-popup-bg);
  display: flex;
  justify-content: center;
  align-items: center;
  z-index: 1000;
}
```

```css
.popup-content {
  position: relative;
  max-width: 90%;
  max-height: 90%;
}

.popup-image {
  max-width: 100%;
  max-height: 90vh;
  object-fit: contain;
}

.popup-close {
  position: absolute;
  top: var(--space-3);
  right: var(--space-3);
  background: none;
  border: none;
  color: white;
  font-size: 1.5rem;
  cursor: pointer;
  transition: color 0.2s;
}
.popup-close:focus {
  outline: 2px solid var(--color-link);
}

.popup-nav {
  position: absolute;
  top: 50%;
  transform: translateY(-50%);
  background: var(--color-popup-button);
  color: white;
  border: none;
  padding: var(--space-3);
```

```css
    font-size: 1.125rem;
    cursor: pointer;
}
.popup-nav:focus {
    outline: 2px solid var(--color-link);
}

.popup-nav.prev {
    left: var(--space-3);
}

.popup-nav.next {
    right: var(--space-3);
}

@media (max-width: 768px) {
    .image-title {
        font-size: 1.2rem;
    }
    .image-gallery {
        grid-template-columns: repeat(auto-fit, minmax(9.375rem, 1fr));
    }
    .image-gallery img {
        height: 9.375rem;
    }
    .dining-guide p {
        margin-block-end: var(--space-0);
    }
    .carousel-item {
        width: 9.375rem;
    }
    .carousel-image {
        height: 6.25rem;
    }
    .carousel-title {
        font-size: 0.75rem;
    }
```

```css
  .popup-content {
    width: 95%;
  }
  .popup-nav {
    padding: var(--space-1);
    font-size: 1rem;
  }
}
/* Accessibility enhancement for ARIA labels and focus */
[aria-label] {
  cursor: pointer;
}
```

AI Prompt

Write comprehensive, production-ready CSS styles for a modern, clean, and readable web page, likely used for travel, itinerary sharing, or park information. These styles should apply to common elements and custom classes as follows:

Spacing and Box Model Best Practices:

Replaces all traditional margin-top, margin-bottom, margin-left, padding-left, etc., with logical properties like margin-block, margin-block-start, margin-block-end, padding-inline, padding-inline-start, and padding-inline-end for lists (ul, ol), paragraphs (p), cards, and all relevant blocks.

Defines a set of utility spacing classes (such as .mb-10, .mt-10, .pt-10, .pt-20, .pb-10, .pb-20) using CSS variables for spacing.

Color Scheme and Variables:

Moves all color properties into :root as CSS variables (e.g., --color-text, --color-link, --color-bg, etc.) and references them throughout the stylesheet.

Typography and Font Handling:

Sets the font-family in :root (or on body) for typographic consistency across all elements.

Uses relative units like rem for spacing, padding, and font sizes.

Implements responsive font scaling using a media query at a breakpoint of max-width: 768px.

Accessibility and a11y Enhancements:

Adds robust focus styles to all interactive elements (a, button, carousel controls, popup controls, etc.) for keyboard navigation, using visible outlines and background changes.

Ensures all navigation and important interactive elements use ARIA labels for accessibility.

Includes selectors for [aria-label] and rules for [aria-hidden="true"] on purely decorative images with pointer-events disabled.

Component-specific Styling:

Styles the following sections: .main-title, .main-description, .day-block, .common-block, .image-gallery, .image-container, .place-details, .carousel, .popup-overlay, etc. with clean, modern layout principles, soft shadows, color, and robust responsive rules.

Uses logical properties for all margin and padding adjustments.

Maintains strong typographic rhythm (e.g., line height), consistently defined in root or body.

Carousel & Popup Styles:

Ensures appropriate sizing for carousel images and controls, with responsive adjustment for the max-width: 768px breakpoint.

Uses relative units, and references color variables for popup overlays and controls.

General Requirements:

The stylesheet should favor maintainability, accessibility, and responsive design.

Provide comments where ARIA attributes and spacing classes might be applied in the markup.

Summary

This ends our coding part of the book. We learned how to use AI to generate code for developing an end-to-end functional web application. You have also seen that, although AI LLM models could do most of the heavy lifting, the architecture, design concepts, and ability to write the right prompt are essential for developing rapidly and with swiftness.

In our last chapter, we will discuss deployment and the future of coding using the vibe coding toolset.

CHAPTER 13

Deployment and Future of Web Development

This is the last chapter of this book. So far, you have learned how to create a modern web application using full-stack development tools. We also learned about the world of AI prompting and how we can use it to build an application from scratch. In this chapter, we will learn two key topics. First, we will learn how to deploy our web application on a cloud platform, and we will end this book talking about vibe coding, where coding could literally be replaced with natural language.

Application Deployment

Once your code is ready, the next step is to push it to a production cloud environment. The following are the steps you need to perform in Vercel before deploying your code. The steps below assume you have created an account in Vercel.

Create Your Team and Project

We have selected the Hobby project, which is perfect to start with for a personal project. Although Hobby has limitations in terms of build size and project size, it is a great way to kick-start your learning process, as it doesn't charge you any money.

Create a Teams with any name. Teams is a collaborative workspace where multiple users can work on a set of projects. It has a robust mechanism of sharing resources and setting permissions. Once done, create the Vercel project, which will hold the build code for our web application. I named the project as **thehalftimewhistle**, which is the website name of the project we built in this book. Your project, once fully configured, will appear like the below screen:

CHAPTER 13   DEPLOYMENT AND FUTURE OF WEB DEVELOPMENT

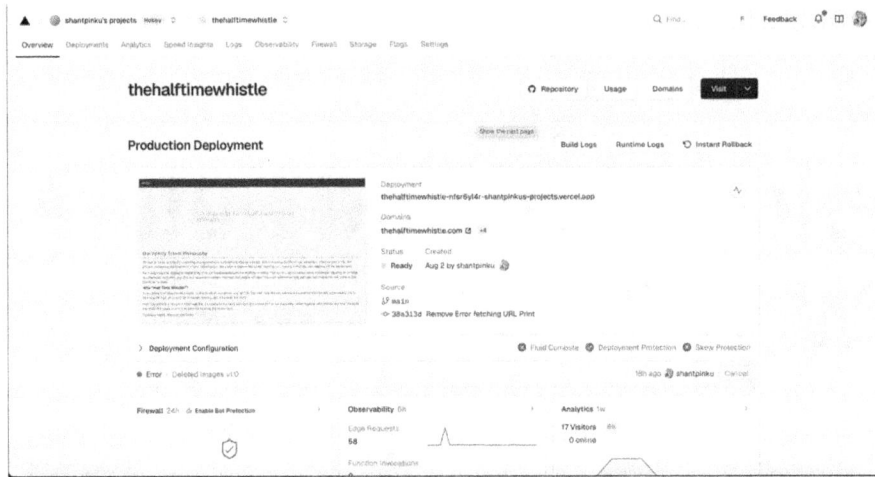

Git Settings

Vercel auto-deploys from a Git repository, by default from the main branch. While creating the project, you need to mention your Git repository details. To look at your Git settings, from the Vercel main menu, navigate to Settings and then select Git from the list of Settings options.

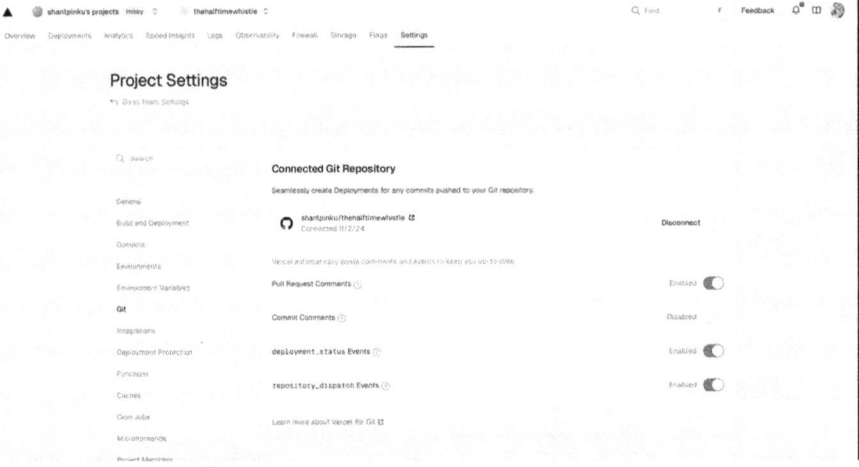

In the Git Settings page, you can enable Git Large File Storage (Git LFS) to manage large files by storing them on the remote GitHub LFS server instead of copying them to Vercel. This optimizes storage usage by keeping only lightweight pointer files in the Git repository while the actual large files reside on GitHub's LFS storage. GitHub manages the LFS storage and automatically configures Git hooks to handle uploading and syncing these large files during Git operations like push. This setup also allows deployment hooks to be triggered on specific branch updates, streamlining the deployment process without burdening the deployment platform with large file storage. The .gitattributes file specifies which file types are tracked via Git LFS, ensuring efficient version control and transfer of large binary files.

Build and Deployment Settings

Vercel can auto-deploy as soon as the code changes in the GitHub repository. In this setting page, you can provide your build command (e.g., npm install and npm run build), mention your Node.js version, and build concurrently. Some of the features are enabled only when you pay.

Please note that Vercel supports a wide range of popular front-end and full-stack frameworks out of the box, including React, Next.js, Nuxt.js, SvelteKit, Remix, Gatsby, and others. Next.js, developed and maintained by Vercel. It seamlessly integrates React with features like server-side rendering, static site generation, and API routes that work without any extra configuration.

Also, Vercel offers key features such as edge caching, which serves static assets from locations closest to users worldwide to minimize latency. It also uses advanced cold start optimizations for serverless functions to ensure functions spin up quickly, reducing delays when traffic surges or when inactive functions are invoked. Additionally, Vercel's incremental static regeneration enables updating content without full redeployments, improving both efficiency and user experience.

CHAPTER 13   DEPLOYMENT AND FUTURE OF WEB DEVELOPMENT

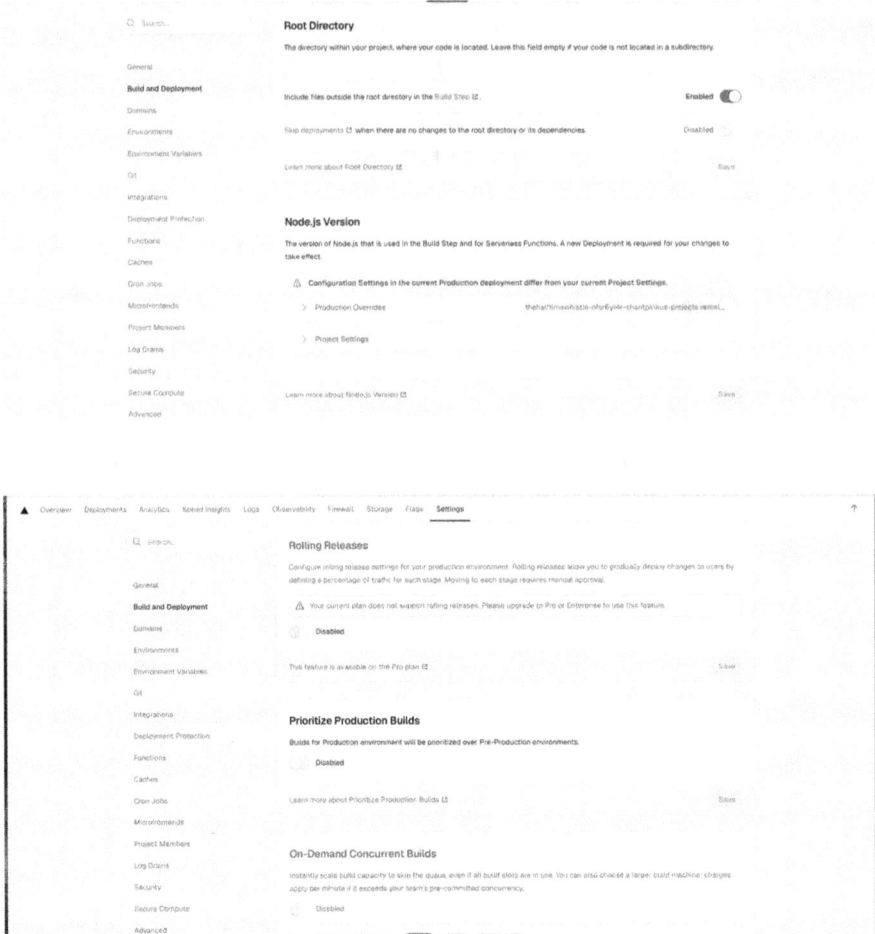

Environment Variables Settings

This is the section where you will define all environment variables for your code to read and perform the necessary action. In our project, we have set two environment variables, one for the MongoDB connection and the other to build the code with no cache. Names of the variables are below:

VERCEL_FORCE_NO_BUILD_CACHE
MONGODB_URI

CHAPTER 13   DEPLOYMENT AND FUTURE OF WEB DEVELOPMENT

Some other examples are

```
DB_URI
DEV_ENV
NEXT_PUBLIC_API_URL
SECRET_KEY
REDIS_HOST
NODE_ENV
```

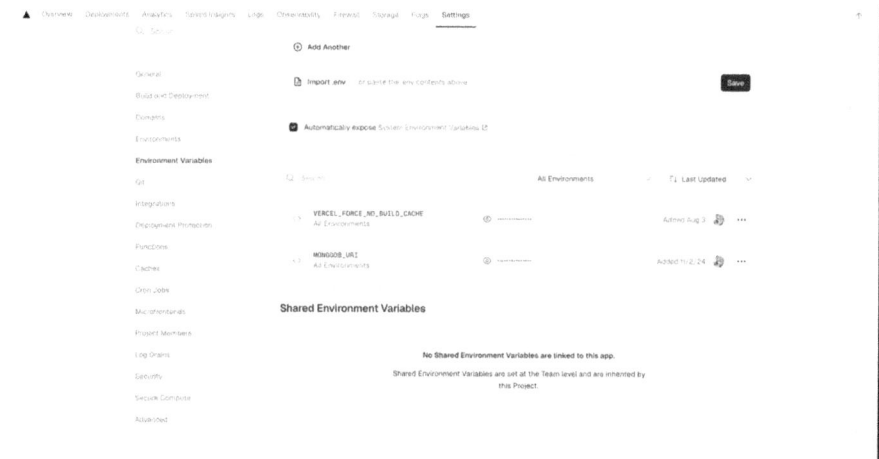

Environment Settings

In your deployment life cycle, you may have different environments such as development, pre-production, and production. In our build, we built everything for production, but a good practice is always to have multiple environments so that you can build, test, and deploy with confidence. This Settings page allows you to set multiple environments to achieve the same.

269

CHAPTER 13   DEPLOYMENT AND FUTURE OF WEB DEVELOPMENT

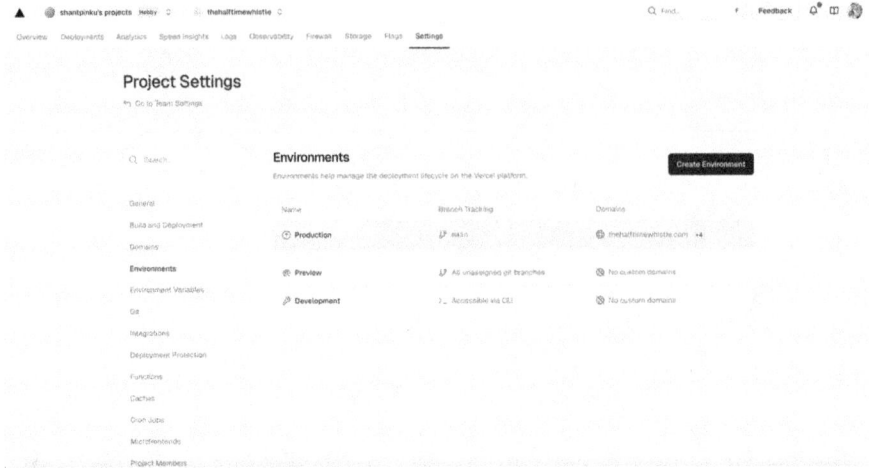

Summary

In this chapter, we learned how to set up our application in Vercel and configure some of the key project settings to ensure a functional product.

This book provided you with a deeper understanding of front-end development using React.js and how to create a fully functional modern web application using AI to accelerate the coding. While most of the code was written by AI, the design of your application and the architectural building blocks were defined by us. We also learned nine different ways to create prompts and utilize some techniques while building this application.

With the advent of vibe coding, building applications is taking a different dimension altogether. Tools such as Cursor, Replit, and Lovable allow us to build web applications rapidly using natural language. As you further enhance your skills to develop web applications, a natural next step would be to use some of these tools to create your next exciting web application.

Happy learning.

Index

A

AI-assisted coding
    ChatGPT, 84
    code completion, 84
    debugging, 84
    documentation, 84
    Gemini, 84
    getting NFR recommendation, 85
    Perplexity, 84
    rapid prototyping, 84

AI prompt, 230
    a11y enhancements, 264
    accessibility, 145, 264
    add example data, 145
    additional requirements, 175
    Carousel & Popup Styles, 264
    clarity for output, 145
    color scheme and variables, 263
    component functionality, 173
    component-specific styling, 264
    context and branding, 145
    CSS
        block card style, 158
        content blocks layout, 157
        featured block, 158
        footer, 159
        header and banner, 157
        hover effects, 159
        main content, 157
        navigation bar, 157
        overall layout, 156
        responsive design, 159
    general requirements, 264
    imports, 173
    JSX structure, 174, 175
    navigation, 145
    prefer snippet-only, 145
    prompt, 143–145
    SEO, 145
    spacing and box model best practices, 263
    structure, 145
    typography and font handling, 263

AI trends, 8

API Route handlers, 112–114

API Routing, 108

App.js
    complete code, 126, 127
    component and routing breakdown, 125, 126
    imports, 124, 125
    MongoDB API Code, AI prompting, 128
    React Router, 124

Application configuration
    App.js, 124–128
    environment default system files, 101
    package.json, 102–107
    package-lock.json, 107, 108
    server.js, 108–122
    Vercel.json, 123, 124

INDEX

Application deployment
    build and deployment settings, 267
    create teams and projects, 265
    environment settings, 269
    environment variables settings, 268
    Git settings, 266

B

Back-end development, 29, 31
Banner image, 135, 146–147
Banner text, 147
BEM, *see* Block Element Modifier (BEM)
Binary JSON (BSON), 22, 44, 45
block-content, 158
Block Element Modifier (BEM), 36
BSON, *see* Binary JSON (BSON)

C

Carousel Styles, 248
Cascading Style Sheets (CSS), 27, 28
    frameworks, 35, 36
    responsive design, 35, 36
Chain-of-thought prompting, 60–62
ChatGPT, 55
CI/CD pipeline, 107
Clickable elements, 249
CMS, *see* Content Management Systems (CMS)
Common block, 239, 240
Complete code, 138–143, 152
Component-based architecture, 39
Content block design, 148–149
content-blocks, 157
ContentDisplayOne, 128, 230
Content Management Systems (CMS), 2, 3

Content Management Web Platform, 2
Content rendition, 217–219, 221–223
Continent page, 161
    AI prompt, 173, 175
    complete code, 168–172
    footer section, 168
    header section, 166
    imports, 162–164
    main content, 167, 168
    metadata management, 165, 166
    navigation component, 164
    region file, 161
CSS, *see* Cascading Style Sheets (CSS)
Cursor, 55, 84, 270
Custom carousel, 71, 76–78, 82, 83

D

Database management, MongoDB, *see* MongoDB
Data encryption, 51
Data fetching, 178
Data persistence, 6, 52, 53
Debugging, 6, 56, 84
Deep learning, 56
Dependency tree, 107
Destinations, 89–92
Detail experience page, 94–95
Detail travel page, 205
    AI prompt, 263, 264
    body, 234
    common block, 239, 240
    complete code, 249–263
    containers, 236–238
    headings, 235
    image gallery, 238, 239
    image styling, 242–249

INDEX

layout, 236–238
list styling, 235, 236
main content display react page
    AI prompt, 230–232
    complete code, 223–227, 229, 230
    content rendition, 217–219, 221–223
    Fetch Content, 211–213
    imports and initializations, 208, 209
    retrieve parameters function, 209, 210
    variable initializations, 213–217
    See also Main content display react page
paragraphs, 235
root, stylesheet, 232, 233
section-specific styles, 240–242
stylesheet, 232
utility spacing, 233
Development environment setup, 11
    GitHub setup
        GitHub Repository creation, 15, 16
        project directory creation, 16
        setup VS Code, 16–18
    installing Git, 12
    installing VS Code, 13–15
    installing Xcode CLT, 11, 12
    MongoDB setup
        Terminal and Homebrew, 22
        using MongoDB Web interface, 19–22

E

Embedded model, 47
Embedding, 46
Environment default system files, 101
Environment variables, 109, 268
ESLint Scripts, 104

Experience pages
    detail, 94, 95
    JSON data structure, 95–99
    summary, 92–94

F

Featured block style, 150–151
Fetch content, 211–213
Few-shot prompting, 57–60
Flat model, 47
Footer design, 151
Footer section, 168
Front-end development, 29, 31
    CSS
        frameworks, 35, 36
        responsive design, 35, 36
    description, 33
    HTML5, 33, 34
    JavaScript, 37, 38
    React.js, 38, 39
    SPA, 41, 42
    state management with Redux, 40, 41
Full-stack development, WordPress and Wix
    flexibility
        control, 30
        future-proof, 31
        optimized performance, 31
        scalability, 30
    limitations
        limits on control, 30
        limits on customization, 30
        performance, 30
        routing challenges, 30
Full-stack frameworks, 3
Full-stack web application, 3, 5, 31
Functional imports, 132

G

GANs, *see* Generative Adversarial Networks (GANs)
Gatsby, 267
Gen AI, *see* Generative AI (Gen AI)
Generated knowledge prompting, 69–70
Generative Adversarial Networks (GANs), 56
Generative AI (Gen AI), 26
    web development
        AI-assisted coding, 84, 85
        AI-generated code, 56
        deep learning, 56
        LLM models, 55
        prompt engineering, 56–83
getImagePath, 221, 222
Getting NFR Recommendation, 85
Git, 12–13, 266–267
GitHub, 15–18, 26, 266
GitHub extension, 14
GitHub Pull Requests and Issues, 14
GitHub Repository, 12, 13, 15–16
Git Large File Storage (Git LFS), 266, 267
Git operations, 267
Git repository, 11, 12, 266
Global Error Handlers, 115
Google, 19, 50, 134

H

Half Time Whistle project, 8, 9
Half Time Whistle web application, 25–27
handleBackClick function, 221
handleBlockClick function, 133, 165
Header & Banner, 157
Header and banner layout, 146
Header section, 166
Hobby project, 265

Home page
    AI prompt, 143, 145, 156–159
    banner image, 147
    banner text, 147
    complete code, 138–143, 152, 154–156
    components, 129
    content block design, 148, 149
    featured block style, 150, 151
    footer design, 151
    header and banner layout, 146
    home page stylesheet, 145
    import statements, 130–132
    main content area, 148
    main page layout, 134–137
    media queries, 152
    meta data and SEO, 133, 134
    navigation bar, 147, 148
    overarching layout, 146
    page navigation, 132, 133
HomePage, 132
Horizontal scroll carousel, 74–75, 83
HTML5, 27, 33–34
HTTPS, 2, 4, 29
Hybrid model, 47
Hypertext Markup Language (HTML), 27, 28
Hypertext Transfer Protocol (HTTP), 29, 108, 109

I

imageBlock array, 221
image-block-carousel, 248
Image container, 248
Image gallery, 238, 239
imageName, 215
Image Path, 215
Image styling, 242–249

Imports
- DOMPurify, 208
- multiple CSS imports, 208
- React imports, 208
- Router hooks, 208

Import statements, 130–132, 164
Instruction-based prompting, 65–68
Intellectual property (IP), 56

J

JavaScript, 28, 37, 38
- description, 28

JSON data structure, 90, 95
JSX, 28, 39, 174

K

Kerberos, 50

L

LangChain, 76
Large language models (LLMs), 3, 56
LDAP, 50
Library-based carousel, 76, 82
List styling, 235–236
LLM models, 55, 60, 63, 65, 76, 177
Logs memory, 115
Lovable, 270

M

macOS, 11, 22
Main content, 148, 157, 167, 168
Main page layout, 134–137
Media queries, 151–152
Metadata management, 165
MongoDB, 18, 26, 45
- active community, 45
- BSON, 44, 45
- cloud native, 43
- cloud native NoSQL, 44
- cloud native solution, 45
- collection, 45
- databases, 45
- database security
  - authentication, 50
  - authorization, 50, 51
  - built-in mechanisms, 50
  - data encryption, 51
- data modeling, 46, 47
- data persistence, 52, 53
- document model, 45
- document-oriented database, 44
- flexible schema design, 44
- horizontally scale, 44
- indexing method, 44
- MQL, 45
- queries are faster, 44
- query optimization
  - avoid over-indexing, 48
  - caching, 49
  - compound indexes, 48
  - creation of indexes, 48
  - explain() method, 49
  - explan() method, 50
  - geospatial indexes, 48
  - index usage, 48
  - multi-key indexes, 48
  - pipeline, 49
  - right data types, 49
  - sharding, 49
  - single field indexes, 48
  - structures, 48, 49
  - text index, 48
- rapid application development, 44

INDEX

MongoDB (*cont.*)
    replication (replica sets), 45
    unique identifier(_id), 45
MongoDB concepts
    collection, 22
    database, 22
    document, 22
MongoDB database, 18, 21, 50, 89, 177
MongoDB Initial Launch Screen, 19
MongoDB Query Language (MQL), 45
Multiple div blocks/sections, 167

N

Navigation bar, 147–148, 157
Navigation component, 164–165
nextImage, 217
Next.js, 267
Node.js version, 105, 267
Nonfunctional requirements (NFR), 63
Nuxt.js, 267

O

OAuth. 19, 50
OpenAI API, 58
Operational and error handling, 114–15
Output formatting/constraint
    prompting, 68–69
Overarching layout, 146

P, Q

package.json configuration file
    about the project, 102, 103
    browser list, 105
    complete code, 105–107
    and dependencies, 102

ESLint Scripts, 104
Node.js version, 105
React Scripts, 103–104
package-lock.json, 107–108
Page layout code, 134
Page navigation, 132–133
Perplexity, 3, 4, 26, 55, 84
PlaceComponent, 183–184, 194
Point-in-time recovery (PITR), 52
pop-up content, 223
prevImage, 217
Project-level imports, 162
Prompt engineering, 4, 8
    chain-of-thought prompting, 60–62
    few-shot prompting, 57–60
    generated knowledge
        prompting, 69, 70
    goals, 56
    instruction-based prompting,
        65–68
    LLMs, 56
    output formatting/constraint
        prompting, 68, 69
    role-play/persona prompting, 62–65
    self-consistency prompting, 71–76
    tree-of-thought prompting, 76–83
    zero-shot prompting, 57

R

React Framework with MongoDB, 3
React.js, 26, 38–39, 71, 104, 134, 270
React Router, 124, 178, 210
React scripts, 103–104
React useState, 212
Redux
    state management, 40, 41
Referenced Model, 47

Region page
    AI prompt, 194, 195
        body, 204
        classes and elements, 202
        hover state for .item, 203
        image inside .item, 203
        .item, 202, 203
        .item-content, 203
        .items-container, 202
        paragraph inside .item, 204
        responsive adjustments (for screens ≤ 768px), 204
        titles inside .item (<h2>), 203
    in block form, 177
    complete code, 188–193
    component definition, 179–181
    components, 177
    concepts, 178
    content render structure, 186–189
    data with useEffect, 181
    fetchPlaces function, 181–183
    imports, 179
    PlaceComponent, 183, 184
    rendering content, 184–186
    stylesheet, 195, 196
    user flow, 178, 179
Remix, 267
Rendering content, 184–186
Replit, 270
Responsive design, 159
Responsive styles, 249
Retrieve parameters function
    location, 209
    originalTitle, 209, 210
    params, 209
    Second Priority, 210
    setRegion, setTitle, setOriginalTitle, 209
    Third Priority, 210
    useEffect, 210
Rich ecosystem, 39
Role-play/persona prompting, 62–65

S

Salted Challenge Response Authentication Mechanism (SCRAM), 45, 50
Schema generation, 119–121
scrollBy, 215
scrollCarousel(), 221
Search Engine Optimization (SEO), 165, 178
Section-specific styles, 240–242
Self-consistency prompting, 71–76
SEO inclusion, 133
server.js
    AI prompting
        errors and omissions, 119
        Get Data from MongoDB, 121, 122
        schema generation, 119–121
    API Route handlers, 112–114
    API routing, 108
    complete code, 115–119
    connecting to back-end databases, 108
    environment, imports and app setup, 109
    faster access to react files, 108
    functions, 108
    HTTP requests, 108
    middleware setup, 109
    MongoDB Connection, 110
    MongoDB schemas and models, 110, 111
    operational and error handling features, 114, 115

server.js (*cont.*)
  optimization, 108
  static file serving, 110
Server Side Rendering (SSR), 92
Single-page application (SPA)
  concept, 41
  cross-platform compatibility, 42
  decoupling front end and back end, 42
  design, 41
  faster loading times, 42
  intuitive user experience, 41
  offline functionality, 42
  reduce server load, 42
Single-Page Architecture (SPA), 31
SSR, *see* Server Side Rendering (SSR)
State management with Redux, 40–41
Static site generation (SSG), 88–89, 267
Stylesheet
  body style, 200
  complete code, 200–202
  container, 196
  designs, 195
  .item-content, 198
  .item h2, 198
  .item:hover, 197, 198
  .item img, 198, 199
  .item p, 199
  principles, 195, 196
  responsive design (Media Query for ≤768px), 199, 200
Summary experience page, 92–94
SvelteKit, 267
System imports, 131–132

T

Text Classes, 248
"The Half Time Travel Website", 143, 173
thehalftimewhistle, 265
thehalftimewhistle.com
  continent, 88, 89
  design and user experience, 99
  destinations, 89–92
  experience pages, 92–99
  home page, 87, 88
Transmission Control Protocol/Internet Protocol (TCP/IP), 29
Travel experiences, 87–100
Tree-of-thought prompting, 76–83
TSL/SSL Certificates, 50

U

useEffect, 179, 181, 194, 210
useEffect hook, 209, 211
useNavigate, 132, 165
Utility spacing, 233

V

Variable initializations, 213–217
Variational Autoencoders (VAEs), 56
Vercel, 26, 265
  build and deployment settings, 267
  create Teams and projects, 265
  environment settings, 269
  environment variables, 268
  Git settings, 266
Vercel.json, 123–124

Virtual DOM, 39
Visual Studio Code (VS Code), 13–15, 26
VS Code GitHub Integration, 17

W

Web application
    AI and prompt engineering, 6
    deployment and optimization, 7
    full-stack application, 6, 7
    web development foundation, 5, 6
    web development future, 7, 8
    web development paradigms, 5

Web development
    CMS, 2, 3
    cutting-edge web applications, 2
    generative AI and prompt engineering, 3
    information-driven static sites, 1
    security considerations, 4

static web applications, 2
Web 1.0, 1
Web 2.0, 1
Web development fundamentals
    back-end development, 29
    core technologies, 27, 28
    front-end development, 29
    understanding core technologies, 28, 29
    web architectures and protocols, 29

X, Y

Xcode Command Line Terminal (CLT), 11, 12
XSS Protection, 188, 195

Z

Zero-shot prompting, 57, 83

GPSR Compliance
The European Union's (EU) General Product Safety Regulation (GPSR) is a set of rules that requires consumer products to be safe and our obligations to ensure this.

If you have any concerns about our products, you can contact us on

ProductSafety@springernature.com

In case Publisher is established outside the EU, the EU authorized representative is:

Springer Nature Customer Service Center GmbH
Europaplatz 3
69115 Heidelberg, Germany